100 Tips using
Windows 8.1 & Office 2013

Nathalie –
So great to meet you
here at NWAIS in Tacoma.
Here's to your success.
Best,

Vickie Sokol Evans, MCT

100 Tips using Windows 8.1 & Office 2013

By Vickie Sokol Evans

Reprinted March 8, 2016

www.**redcapeco**.com

PUBLISHED BY
The Red Cape Company, LLC
9901 Brodie Lane, Suite 160-225
Austin, TX 78748

support@redcapeco.com

Author: Vickie Sokol Evans, MCT

Technical Editors: Anita Evans and Mandi Woodroof

Microsoft, Microsoft Press, Access, ActiveX, Excel, Expression, Groove, InfoPath, Internet Explorer, OneNote, OpenType, Outlook, PivotTable, PowerPoint, SharePoint, SkyDrive, SmartArt, Visio, Windows, Windows Live, Windows Mobile, Windows Server, Windows Vista, and Office 365 are either registered trademarks or trademarks of the Microsoft group of companies. Other product and company names mentioned herein may be the trademarks of their respective owners.

The example companies, organizations, products, domain names, email addresses, logos, people, places, and events depicted herein are fictitious. No association with any real company, organization, product, domain name, email address, logo, person, place, or event is intended or should be inferred.

This manual expresses the author's views and opinions. The information contained in this manual is provided without any express, statutory, or implied warranties. Neither the author, The Red Cape Company, LLC, nor its resellers, or distributors will be held liable for any damages caused or alleged to be caused either directly or indirectly by this manual.

Information contained in this manual has been obtained by The Red Cape Company, LLC from sources believed to be reliable. However, because of the possibility of error by our sources, The Red Cape Company, LLC, or others, do not guarantee the accuracy, adequacy, or completeness of any information and is not responsible for any errors or omissions or the results obtained from use of such information. Readers should be particularly aware of the fact that the Internet is an ever-changing entity. Some facts may have changed since this manual went to press.

Contents

About the icons used in this Guide

 Highlight this. You may want to refer back to it later.

 Look closely. Here is a behind the scenes look at this tip. Read on for helpful information about the tip.

 New. There is something about the tip that was introduced in latest version of Microsoft Office. Read more about the new functionality.

 Reuse, Repeat or Repurpose. Repeat the steps as necessary or reuse the tip for other tasks.

 Stop. In the name of love. If you go any further bad things might happen. Follow the steps provided to help you avoid a problem.

 Save time. There's even a quicker way to use this tip.

 Setting. This provides information required for a specific setting within the application.

 **MOS objective.** The tip meets an objective of a Microsoft Office Specialist certification exam.

 Windows 7. The steps are different for previous versions. Follow the steps if you are using Windows 7.

 **Microsoft Office 2007.** The steps are different for previous versions. Follow these steps if you are using Microsoft Office 2007.

 **Microsoft Office 2010.** The steps are different for previous versions. Follow these steps if you are using Microsoft Office 2010

Windows 8.1

Minimum time saved: 5 minutes

Look, Ma! No mouse.

Many of the tips in this section use a special button on the keyboard known as the Windows logo key, shown in Figure 1 below.

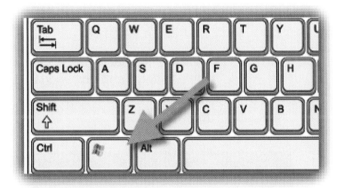

Figure 1. Windows logo key on a standard keyboard

 The Windows logo key will be referred to as the [WINDOWS] key.

Tip #1 Navigate the three main areas of Windows 8.1 using your keyboard

Applies to Windows 8.1

The three areas of the Windows 8.1 environment where you will frequent the most are the Start Screen, All Apps view, and the beloved Desktop. Learn what each of these views do and how to get to them quickly using a keyboard shortcut. And be sure to check out Tip # 5 on how to access them on a touch screen.

Go to …	Purpose	Keyboard Shortcut
Start Screen	What was the vertical Start menu on the left side of the Windows screen in previous editions is now horizontal across our screen (as seen in Figure 1) and fully customizable so that you can put all of your favorite shortcuts, documents, and apps.	[WINDOWS] Key
All Apps	This is the place where all of your Apps are stored.	[CTRL]+[TAB]
Desktop	This is the familiar desktop from previous versions and is where your desktop apps are run.	[WINDOWS] +[D]

Figure 2. Windows 8.1 Start Screen

Tip #2   Save time (and your sanity) by using essential Windows 8 keyboard shortcuts

Applies to Windows 7, Windows 8.1

Yes! That floating Windows Logo key button on your keyboard actually serves a purpose. Who knew!?

Check out these cool shortcuts and timesaving Windows hotkeys that you won't want to live without.

Action	Keyboard Shortcut	When using a mouse
View Explorer Window (My computer window)	[WINDOWS]+[E]	Move mouse pointer to the bottom left hand corner of screen and right-click the Start button. Then choose **File Explorer**.
View Desktop	[WINDOWS]+[D]	Click the Desktop tile on your Start Screen
View Start Screen	[WINDOWS] Key	Move mouse pointer to bottom left hand corner of screen
Cycle through open windows	[WINDOWS]+[TAB]	Swipe in from the left edge of the screen
Open the Charms	[WINDOWS]+[C]	Move mouse to any corner on the right side of your screen
Show the commands for an app	[WINDOWS]+[Z]	Swipe in from the top or bottom edge of the screen
All Apps	[CTRL]+[Tab]	Click the arrow near the lower-left corner of the Start screen
Lock the computer	[WINDOWS]+[L]	
Shut Down or Sign Out	[WINDOWS]+[X]	Right-click the Start button and choose **Shut down or sign out**

Other super productive [Windows] Key shortcuts

Action	Keyboard Shortcut	When using a mouse
View windows side by side using Windows Snap	[WINDOWS]+[RIGHT ARROW] or [WINDOWS]+[LEFT ARROW]	Drag the top of the active window to the right side of your screen to snap in place. Then drag the top of the next active window to the left side of your screen.
Maximize a window quickly	[WINDOWS]+[UP ARROW]	Drag the top of a window to the top of your screen.
Search your computer for documents or emails	[WINDOWS]+[F]	Open the Charms by moving your mouse to any corner on the right side of your screen. Then click Search. Change the drop down to just Files.
Search for everything!	[WINDOWS]+[S]	Open the Charms by moving your mouse to any corner on the right side of your screen. Then click Search.
Create a Note in OneNote	[WINDOWS]+[N]	
Connect to a projector	[WINDOWS]+[P]	

Tip #3   Quickly launch a program

Applies to Windows 7, Windows 8.1

Using your mouse to launch Word, Excel or PowerPoint can be tedious, especially in the new Windows 8.1 environment where nothing looks the same as before. Check out how easy it is to launch any program using the [Windows] key. Why didn't they think of this sooner?

To quickly launch a program

1. Press the [WINDOWS] button. This takes you back to the Start Screen as seen in Figure 3.
2. Next, simply start typing the program you want and the Search pane will display possible matches. It's like magic!

Figure 3. Window 8.1 Start Screen

 You can use this trick to launch all sorts of things: Excel (type: **excel**), Word (type: **word**), PowerPoint (type: **powerpoint**), Games folder (type: **games**), your Printers window (type: **printer**), your music folder (type: **music**), and more...

Tip #4   Close a Window or Application

One of the commands I miss the most when I transitioned from Windows 7 to Windows 8 was the Close command. How do I close my applications and windows? Thankfully, the legacy shortcut still works in Windows 8. Then check Tip #7 below on how to close a Window using the touch screen

To close a window or application

☐ Use the [Alt]+[F4] keyboard shortcut or move your mouse to the top right hand corner of your window.

Use your Touch Screen.

Tip #5 Navigate the three main areas of Windows 8.1 using your touch screen

Applies to Windows 8.1 + Touch Screen

The three areas of the Windows 8.1 environment where you will frequent the most are the Start Screen, All Apps view, and the beloved Desktop. Learn what each of these views do and how to get to them quickly using your touch screen. And be sure to check out Tip # 1 on how to access them using keyboard shortcuts.

Go to …	Purpose	Touch Screen
Start Screen	What was the vertical Start menu on the left side of the Windows screen in previous editions is now horizontal across our screen and fully customizable.	Swipe from right side to view the Charms, then tap Start
All Apps	This is the place where all of your Apps are stored.	Tap and hold the middle of your Start screen and slide up Or with your mouse: click the arrow right above your Start button.
Desktop	This is the familiar desktop from previous versions and is where your desktop apps are run.	Tap the Desktop tile on the Start Screen

Tip #6   Switch between open applications using your touch screen

Applies to Windows 8.1 + Touch Screen

Chances are, if you are working in Windows 8.1 all day, you probably have many apps open. You can easily use your touch screen to switch between the apps you have open.

To cycle through open apps using your touch screen

▨ Swipe from the left side of your screen. Repeat as necessary to cycle through your open apps.

To view all of the open applications

▨ Swipe in from the left edge, and with your finger still on the screen, move it back toward the left edge

In Windows 7, you can toggle back and forth between two windows by pressing [ALT]+[TAB] once, and then repeat. This takes you to the previous window you were using. Press [ALT]+[TAB] again and it takes you back to the other window. Repeat as necessary.

Tip #7   Close a file or program using your touch screen

Applies to Windows 8.1 + Touch Screen

As I mentioned in Tip #4, I had a hard time figuring out how to close an app. I think this tip is so important, I wanted to show you an alternative way to close an app, especially if you're using a touch screen device.

To close a window or app using your touch screen

▨ Drag the app from the top edge of the screen to the bottom of the screen as if you are pulling down a window shade.

Tip #8   View the Charms using your touch screen

Applies to Windows 8.1 + Touch Screen Monitor

Charms are tools to help you manage, find and share your work. They are displayed on a vertical bar on the right hand side of your screen as seen in Figure 4. The five charms: Search, Share, Start, Devices, and Settings are always on the right side of your screen and are just a swipe away.

Figure 4. Charms

To view the Charms

▨ Swipe in from the right side of your screen.

Tip #9   Access commands for apps and items using your touch screen

Applies to Windows 8.1 + Touch Screen Monitor

When you need to access commands for applications and files that were once available in the menus and toolbars and shortcut menus, you can now view them at the top or bottom of an app. Here's how.

To view commands using a Touch Screen

Action	Touch Screen	Mouse
See commands for an app	Swipe from bottom or from top	Right-click the app
Commands for items	Swipe up and down on an item (like pictures) to view the commands for the picture Swipe left/right on an item (like email) to view the commands for the email.	Right-click the item
In desktop	Press and hold an item to see the shortcut menu	Right-click the item

Personalize your experience.

Tip #10 Pin your favorite apps to the Start Screen

Applies to Windows 8.1

In previous version of Windows, the Start Menu was a vertical list of applications and tools that served as our own command central. Now in Windows 8, our Start Menu has become the Start Screen with more real estate and a fully customizable experience. Follow these instructions to create your own unique Start Screen.

To pin your favorite program to the Start Screen

1. Navigate to the Start Screen by clicking the [WINDOWS] key or clicking the Windows icon in the bottom left hand corner of your screen.
2. Use [CTRL]+[TAB] to view all your apps.
3. Using your mouse, right-click the application you wish to make a shortcut for (or on your touch screen, press and hold the application) to view the Customize bar.
4. Then click **Pin to Start** as shown in Figure 5.

Figure 5 Pin to Start

To pin your favorite program to the Taskbar on your Desktop

1. Repeat steps 1-3 above.
2. Then click **Pin to Taskbar**.

 Your pinned Taskbar items are in the order in which you pinned them. If you want to change the order you can move them around. Simply drag a pinned item before or after the other pinned items.

 If the program is running, right-click the program button on the taskbar and click Pin to taskbar.

Tip #11 Create a shortcut to your favorite people, sites, and documents

Applies to Windows 8.1

In the previous step you added your favorite apps to the Start Screen. The next step is to add your favorite people, websites and files.

To pin your favorite people to your Start Screen

1. Find the person in your People App on your Start Screen. If you can't find the People App, use [WINDOWS]+[S] and type **People**.
2. Once you find the person, using your mouse, right-click anywhere on the person to get the command menu or using your touch screen, swipe from the bottom of your screen to get the commands, or use the shortcut [WINDOWS]+[Z].
3. Click **Pin to Start**.

To pin your favorite websites to your Start Screen

1. Go to your favorite web page.
2. Once you find the webpage, using your mouse, right-click anywhere on the person to get the command menu or using your touch screen, swipe from the bottom of your screen to get the commands, or use the shortcut [WINDOWS]+[Z].
3. Click or tap the Star button and then click or tap **Pin to Start**.

To pin your favorite folders to your Start Screen

1. Navigate to your folders [WINDOWS]+[E] or click the Desktop icon and browse your folders).
2. Using your mouse, right-click the folder to get the command menu or using your touch screen, tap and hold to get the command menu.
3. Click or tap **Pin to Start**.

Tip #12 Move tiles around, group and rename

Now that you've added your favorite apps, people, websites and folders, it's time to move them around, group and rename them and customize your Start Screen just right.

To begin customizing the Start Screen, you must always be on the Start Screen.

To move tiles around the Start Screen

- Using your Touch Screen: Tap and drag the tile to the desired location.
- Using a mouse: Drag and drop the tile to the desired location.

To group tiles

You can group a set of tiles together.

1. Using your mouse, drag and drop a tile in between two established groups or to the end and drop it when you see a vertical bar indicating the new group position. Using your touch screen, simply tap and hold to drag the tile to the right position.
2. Then add more tiles to the group directly below the first tile or to the right of the tile.
3. Repeat as necessary.

To move groups

1. Zoom out as described below, so that you have a bird's eye view of the groups.
2. Tap and drag or click and drag the group of tiles you want to move to where you want it to go.
3. Once you're done moving groups, tap or click anywhere on the screen to zoom back in.

To name the groups

1. Use [Ctrl]+[Z] to view the commands for the Start Screen.
2. Click Customize, to see the Group Names at the top of the groups.

3. Click in the group name box to rename.

To zoom in and out

To Zoom in or out of anything on Windows, including the Start Screen, here are the steps

- Keyboard short: Ctrl+ or Ctrl-
- Mouse: Press Ctrl while you rotate the wheel button or click the zoom button in the lower right hand corner of your Start Screen (at the end of the scroll bar). Then click the Start Screen to zoom back in.
- Touch Screen: Pinch the start screen or stretch to zoom in

Office 2013

Use Office anywhere, anytime, on any device.

Tip #13 Sign in to Office using your Microsoft ID

New in Office 2013

What kind of super human benefit is there to signing in to Office 2013? Well, just like those famous superheroes, you get to work whenever and wherever you want! Signing in to Office 2013 allows you to save your Office files securely online and access them anywhere, anytime and share with anyone. Even better, your favorite themes and settings travel with you—even across different devices.

To sign in to Office 2013

1. After installing Office 2013 you will be prompted to sign in with your Microsoft ID. If you don't have a Microsoft ID use your favorite email address to create your Microsoft ID.
2. Type in your account email address and press **Next**, as shown in Figure 6.
3. Once signed in your name will display in the upper right-hand corner of the program window, under the Minimize, Restore and Exit buttons.
4. If the name displayed is incorrect, click the drop down arrow and click **Switch Account**. The login screen will appear letting you sign into your account.

Figure 6 Sign in to Microsoft Account

Tip #14 Save your files to OneDrive for anytime, anywhere access

Applies to Office 2010, Office 2013

When you find yourself working on a different computer and need access to a document or important presentation, there's nothing more frustrating than realizing that you have to be on a specific computer to get that file. Never fear, OneDrive is here! Formerly called SkyDrive, OneDrive is your secure cloud-based file storage so that you're never without your files. Additionally, you'll be able to share those files and collaborate easily using the familiar Office applications.

Because you set up a Microsoft ID in the previous tip, you already have OneDrive with plenty of storage space. For more information, visit OneDrive.com.

Additionally, if you are using SharePoint 2013, you also have OneDrive for Business, which is where you can store all of your work that may not need to be shared. This is a GREAT alternative to saving to the Desktop, Documents folder or Network folder because you can access them from any device.

Let's take a look at the OneDrive locations I use to save my files.

Figure 7. Office 2013 Save Locations

	Command	Description
1	The Red Cape Company, LLC	This is my corporate SharePoint account where I can save my documents to various Team Sites on my company's Intranet. For internal documents only.
2	OneDrive @ The Red Cape Company, LLC	This is my OneDrive for Business account where I can save all of my work-related files in the cloud that I may or may not share with my colleagues. For internal documents only.
3	Vickie's OneDrive	This is my test account for OneDrive. I only use this for testing and training purposes. You can ignore this one for now.

	Command	Description
4	Vickie Sokol Evans's OneDrive	This is where I save all of my personal files as well as any public files that I want to share. It's similar to a DropBox or Google Drive account but much easier to use because it is inherent with Microsoft Office.
5	Other Web Locations	This is where you can pin favorite locations.
6	Computer	This is the native My Computer location where you can save to your Desktop or Documents or even a network drive.
7	Add a Place	If none of the options above work for you, you can always specify an exact online file drive here.

To save your files to OneDrive

1. From the **File** tab, click **Save As**. Because you have signed in using your Microsoft ID, you should see your available locations. If not, you may need to sign in.

Share your document with friends and colleagues by saving it to OneDrive and inviting them to view it.

2. Select your OneDrive account.
3. Choose a location in your OneDrive folders.
4. Type a file name, and then click **Save**.

Tip #15 Access Office files on your tablet or mobile device

Applies to Office Online

There is a free, online version of Microsoft Office that has been available since Office 2010, called Office Online. Office Online means that we can use Word, Excel and PowerPoint (as well as OneNote) in any browser! Because it's available in the browser, this means that we can use it on any device that has a browser: your phone, your table, or your laptop. And some devices have Microsoft Office apps such as the Windows phone, Surface tablet, and now iPads. So no matter where you are, you can find and edit that important document or spreadsheet and deliver professional results fast!

Note: to use Office on your iPad, you must have a subscription to Office 365, which for a low monthly fee, gives you full licenses to Office to use on up to five devices, regardless of the platform (i.e. PC and/or Mac).

Access Office files on your table or mobile device using your browser

1. If you have the link to your SharePoint or OneDrive document (perhaps in an email or saved to your phone/tablet), simply click on the link and sign in, if necessary. Otherwise, log into your OneDrive or SharePoint account and locate the document.
2. Once you find the document in your cloud account, open the document in your browser to view it as seen in Figure 8.

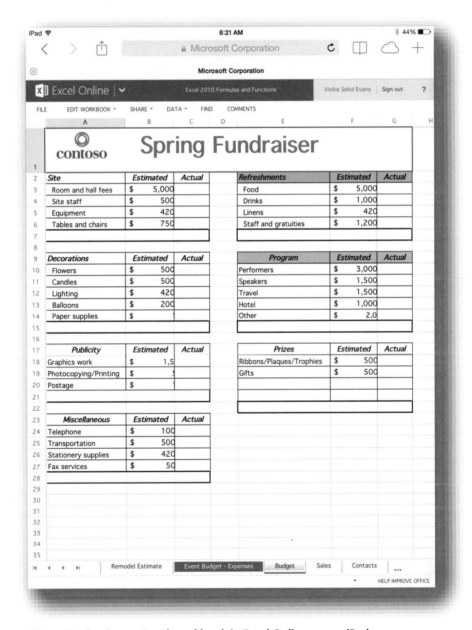

Figure 8. Viewing an Excel workbook in Excel Online on my iPad

3. To edit the file, click on **Edit Workbook** on the toolbar (or Edit Document or Edit Presentation depending on what program you're using) as seen in Figure 9.

4. **No need to worry about saving changes!** All changes you make in the browser are automatically saved. Simply close the browser to get out of your document.

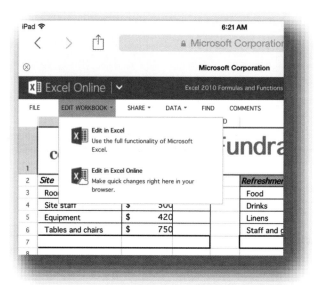

Figure 9. Editing options for Excel Online

Tip #16 Use Ribbon Display options to manage the real estate on your screen

New in Office 2013

A new button has joined the group in the upper right-hand corner of Office 2013 called Ribbon Display Options as seen in Figure 10.

Figure 10. Ribbon Options and Collapse Ribbon buttons.

It provides an easier access for touch screen users to control the functionality of the ribbon. Whether you have touch screen or if you're using a mouse, you can do the following:

- Auto-hide the ribbon
- Show tabs only
- Show tabs and commands

To change how the Ribbon is displayed

1. Click the Ribbon Display Options button on the top right-hand corner of the Ribbon as seen in Figure 10.
2. Then select the option of your choice.

Minimize the Ribbon

Applies to Office 2007, Office 2010, Office 2013

In Office 2013 you can still double-click on any tab to hide the commands on the ribbon, but not to hide the tabs themselves. Or you can use the Collapse Ribbon button to hide the ribbon.

To minimize the ribbon

- Click the arrow in the bottom right hand corner of the ribbon to minimize the ribbon.

To pin a collapsed Ribbon

1. Click on a ribbon tab to expand the ribbon.
2. In the bottom right-hand corner of the ribbon, click the pin icon.

Access shortcut keys to commands on the Ribbon

Applies to Office 2007, Office 2010, Office 2013

Calling all keyboard junkies! If you relied on the [ALT] keyboard shortcuts to access menus and commands back in Office 2003, then you were probably disappointed when you could no longer use the same [ALT] keystrokes in Office 2007 or 2010.

However, the good news is that you can cheat your way back to the head of the class using Key Tips. The even BETTER news is that the old [ALT] keystrokes from Office 2003 work in Office 2010 and Office 2013. Whew, I'm exhausted with excitement!

To activate the Key Tips available for the new ribbons and commands

- Press [ALT] on your keyboard (as seen in Figure 11) and then press the corresponding letter for the Ribbon or toolbar button. Keep pressing the letters you see on screen until it launches the command you need.

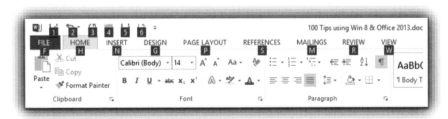

Figure 11. Key Tips activated

Tip #17 Create your own toolbar

Applies to Office 2007, Office 2010, Office 2013

If you like to customize your toolbars, then good news! You can customize the Quick Access Toolbar to display any command you want. The default location for the Quick Access Toolbar is in the top left-hand corner of your Microsoft Office window right above the File and Home tabs as shown in Figure 12. You get three default buttons for each of the Office applications: Save, Undo, and Redo. But let's see how you can easily add more of your favorite commands.

Figure 12. Quick Access Toolbar

To add a Ribbon command to your Quick Access Toolbar

▪ Right-click any command on the Ribbon and choose **Add to Quick Access Toolbar**.

To add a command to your Quick Access Toolbar that ISN'T on the Ribbon

1. Click the drop-down arrow on the right-hand side of the Quick Access Toolbar. Choose from the list of popular commands. Otherwise, click More Commands.
2. In the **Choose commands from:** list, (see item 1 in Figure 13), click the dropdown arrow to select a category of commands. To view all

commands alphabetically, choose **All Commands** from the dropdown list.

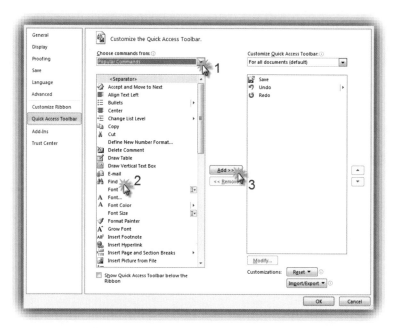

Figure 13. Customize Quick Access Toolbar Window

3. Select the command you want from the list on the left (see item 2 in Figure 13).

4. Click the **Add >>** button (see item 3 in Figure 13) to add the command to the Quick Access Toolbar list of commands on the right side of the window.

5. Repeat steps 2-4 for each command you wish to add to the Quick Access Toolbar.

6. Click **Ok**.

 You can rearrange the commands you added by using the up and down buttons on the right-hand side of the Customize Quick Access Toolbar window in Figure 13. Be sure to highlight the command before you click the move buttons.

The Quick Access Toolbar can be positioned either above (by default) or below the ribbon. To move it below the ribbon, right-click the Quick Access Toolbar and choose **Show toolbar below the ribbon**.

To move it back above the Ribbon, right-click the Quick Access toolbar and choose **Show toolbar above the ribbon**.

 When a command is no longer a favorite you can remove it by right-clicking the command on the Quick Access Toolbar and choose **Remove from Quick Access Toolbar**.

Work together.

Tip #18 Use New Read Mode in Word & PowerPoint

New in Office 2013

In today's workplace, it is becoming more common to view Office documents on mobile devices such as smartphones and tablets. Because of this, Microsoft has introduced a new view in Office 2013, called Read Mode. See it in action!

Use New Read Mode in Word & PowerPoint

1. With a Word document or PowerPoint file open, go to the **View** tab, in the **Views** group, click **Read Mode**.
2. If you have a touch screen on your monitor or are using your mobile device, simply swipe to view the pages.
3. To get out of Read Mode, use [ESC] on your keyboard.

Tip #19 Reply to comments in the document

New in Office 2013

Reviewing and editing documents is now easier than ever by being able to reply to comments within a document or presentation as you are collaborating with colleagues.

In this example, we are going to add comments to a presentation.

Reply to comments in a document

1. Click the location on the slide where you want to add a comment or simply just click the slide if the comment applies to the entire slide.
2. On the **Review** tab, in the **Comments** group, click **New Comment** and enter your comment.
3. If necessary, click Show Comments.
4. Notice that there is now a new Reply text box underneath your comment. When your colleague sees your comment and wants to

respond, he or she can reply directly to the comment so that you know exactly what they are responding to!

5. Use the commands in the **Review** tab, **Comments** group to modify and delete comments throughout the presentation.

Tip #20 Share files effortlessly with others even if they don't have Office

Applies to Office 2013

When you are ready to send your file to a colleague, instead of sending the file as an attachment, which creates a separate copy of the document, simply share the document with them so that you're both able to work in one document without worrying about who has the latest version. The file will always be the latest version!

If they don't have Word or Excel or PowerPoint, the document opens automatically in Word Online, Excel Online or PowerPoint Online. It's so easy!

Share your document with others

1. Click **File** > **Share** > **Invite People**.

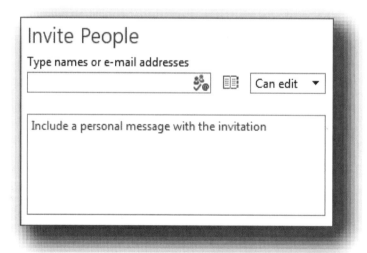

2. Add their email addresses.
3. Click **Share**.

Tip #21 Edit a document with a colleague at the same time

Applies to Office 2010, Office 2013

Many times, if not most of the time, we need the help of our colleagues to complete or review a sales proposal or big presentation. The traditional way of emailing the document back and forth is so inefficient and can cause delays in getting the project done, not to mention cause mistakes, because the two of you are working in separate documents. It's challenging to know who has the latest version and if you're both making changes at the same time, not only are you potentially doing double work, but you then have to take the time to compare documents and merge changes. Just thinking about all that work makes me want to quit the project.

A better, more collaborative way to work is to edit the document together at the same time. Or edit the same exact document but at different times. Either way, you and your colleague are both working in the latest version of the document versus copies of the document and you can ensure that anytime you access the document, you are in the latest and greatest version.

It's the best way to work and to focus on what matters most, which is producing the best the content and delivering professional results fast.

Prerequisite: The file must be stored somewhere in the cloud such as on SharePoint (your Intranet) or in OneDrive as demonstrated in Tip #14.

Edit a document together with a colleague at the same time

1. Save your document in a SharePoint library or in a OneDrive folder.
2. Share the document by going to **File** > **Share** > **Invite People**. If you're document is already closed and saved in SharePoint or OneDrive, do the following:
   a. To share a document in a SharePoint 2013 library, select the document and on the **Files** tab, in the **Share & Track** group, click **Share**.
   b. To share a document stored in OneDrive, select the document and on the top navigation bar click **Share** and complete the information.

3. Once everyone has the link, simply click the link and begin editing the document. If you're both in the document at the same time you will see that there are two authors as seen in Figure 14 and Figure 15.

Figure 14. Two editors in Word 2013 - Status bar indicator

Figure 15. Two editors in Word Online - Upper right-hand corner of browser

4. Make your changes and save regularly so that other people will be able to see your edits. Your edits must be saved first, and the other person must save the document in order to see your edits. And vice versa. If you want to see their edits, they have to save them to the file and then you'll have to save as well to refresh the document.

When two (or more) people are editing the same document, paragraphs will be locked when someone else is editing that paragraph. Repeat step 4 when you want to refresh everyone's edits.

Brand your documents, spreadsheets and presentations.

Tip #22 Globally change the font for your document

Applies to Office 2007, Office 2010, Office 2013

Experts say that you should limit the number of fonts in your document or presentation (and spreadsheet as well) to only two fonts. You should have one font type for your headings and another font for the body text. It's ok to have one font for both headings and body text but you certainly don't want to have a third font.

The traditional way of changing fonts is to select all your text in your document and use the Font drop down box to switch to a new font. The new and improved way is to set the font at the Theme level. Themes are explained in detail in Tip #22. Meanwhile, here's the correct way to globally change your font.

To globally change the font in your document

In Microsoft Word...

1. Without selecting anything, go to the **Design** tab, in the **Document Formatting** group, click the arrow for **Fonts**.
2. Choose one of the Font Sets or create your own (see Tip #23).

In Microsoft Excel...

1. Without selecting anything, go to the **Page Layout** tab, in the **Themes** group, click the arrow for **Fonts**.
2. Choose one of the Font Sets or create your own (see Tip #23).

In Microsoft PowerPoint...

1. On the **Design** tab, in the **Variants** group, click the dropdown arrow and select **Fonts**.
2. Select the font set you want, which will update the Slide Master and its layouts with the correct heading and body fonts.

Tip #23 Create your own Font Set

Applies to Office 2007, Office 2010, Office 2013

If the standard list of Font Sets described in the previous tip don't meet your needs, then you can easily create your own font set to use throughout all of your documents, spreadsheets and presentations.

Create your own Font Set

- Using the Font Set drop down (see steps above) click **Customize Fonts** and identify the font for your Headings and Body Text, then give your Font Set a name such as the name of your company, such as **ABC Company**.

Tip #24 Change the color palette for text, tables and other objects

Applies to Office 2007, Office 2010, Office 2013

Word 2013 makes it easier to find and change the settings for the default color palette in your documents. This means that your text, graphics and tables will match your corporate branding using an expanded list of color options for Office 2013.

To change the color palette of your document

1. Click the **Design** tab.
2. Click the **Colors** icon in the **Document Formatting** group to view the color palettes available.
3. Hover your mouse over different color palettes to preview the look of your document.
4. Click the palette to apply it to the document's contents.

In Office 2007 and Office 2010, on the **Page Layout** tab, in the **Themes** group, select the **Colors** button to view the available color palettes.

 This tip meets the "Applying Page Layout and Reusable Content" objective of the Microsoft® Office Specialist exams for Word.

Tip #25 Brand your documents using Themes

Applies to Word 2007, Word 2010, Word 2013

To extend your brand even further beyond just colors as demonstrated in Tip #22, you can use Office Themes, which include colors, fonts and graphic effects. This allows you to create a consistent and professional-looking document with minimal effort.

To change your document theme

1. On the **Design** tab, at the beginning **Document Formatting** group, select the **Themes** button to view the available Office themes.
2. Hover the mouse over a Theme to get a preview of how your document would look.
3. Click to select the one you want to apply.

 In Office 2007 and Office 2010, on the **Page Layout** tab, in the **Themes** group, select the **Themes** button to view the available Office themes.

 This tip meets the "Applying Page Layout and Reusable Content" objective of the Microsoft® Office Specialist exams for Word.

Tip #26 Create, email and now CONVERT PDFs!

Applies to Office 2007, Office 2010, Office 2013

Woohoo! No more third party tools needed to save your Office document to a PDF. Since Office 2007, you can save any Word, Excel or PowerPoint file as a PDF and my ultimate favorite…instead of saving a file as a PDF, you can email a file as a PDF, which allows you to bypass the saving process and eliminate all of those random PDF files you have on your hard drive or network drive.

I bet you're wondering, "Yeah, but can you convert a PDF back into a document?"

You can now, in Office 2013!

You asked. Microsoft delivered. New in Office 2013 is the ability to convert your PDF back into a Word document so that you can edit a PDF in Word.

Create a PDF

First, let's see how to save a file as a PDF as well as send a PDF (without having to save to your hard drive.)

Save a file as PDF

1. On the **File** tab, click **Export**.
2. Click **Create PDF/XPS Document** as seen in Figure 16.

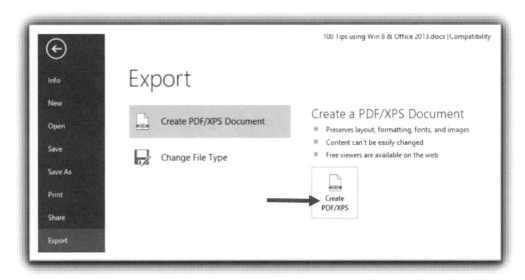

Figure 16. Backstage Window - Create a PDF using Export

To save a file as a PDF in Office 2007 and Office 2010, click the Office button and choose **Save As**. Then click **PDF or XPS**.

This tip meets the "Sharing and Maintaining Documents" objective of the Microsoft® Office Specialist exams for Word, Excel® 2010, and PowerPoint® 2010.

Email a file as a PDF

Applies to Office 2007, Office 2010, Office 2013

Ever since Office 2007 launched, we could now save our documents in PDF format without needing a third party tool. But the challenge with creating so many PDFs is that now we're keeping track of two "file types" for the one document: one in its original format (docx, xlsx, pptx) and the second one as a PDF. Hmm. That just won't do. If you need to email a copy of your file to someone in PDF you can simply email the file as a PDF and bypass the save step altogether.

To email a document as a PDF

1. On the **File** tab, click **Share**.
2. Click **Email** as seen in Figure 16, then click **Send as PDF**.

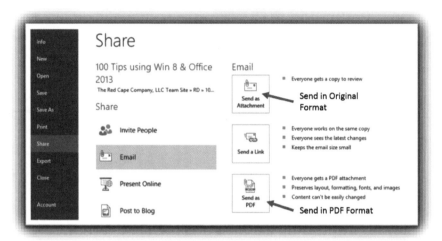

Figure 17. Backstage Window: Email as a PDF

 To email a document as a PDF in Office 2007, click the Office button and choose **Send**. Then click **Email as PDF Attachment**.

 To email a document as a PDF in Office 2010, click **File**, then **Save and Send**. Then click **Send Using Email**, then click **Send as PDF**.

 This tip meets the "Sharing and Maintaining Documents" objective of the Microsoft® Office Specialist exams for Word, Excel® and PowerPoint®.

Convert a PDF to a Word document

New in Office 2013

1. In Word, from the **File** tab, click **Open**.
2. Navigate to your PDF file.
3. Select the PDF file and click **Open**.
4. Click **Ok** if you get the "This may take a while" message.
5. Make changes to the file.
6. To save back to a PDF, from the **File** tab, click **Save As**.
7. Once you find the location where you want to save the document, be sure to select **PDF** from the **Save as type**, otherwise Word will want to save it as a Word document by default.

Tip #27 Remove personal data

Applies to Office 2007, Office 2010, Office 2013

Before you share you document with others, you may want to remove personal data contained in the document such as the author's name (which may or may not be you), editing time, customer information, etc, especially if it isn't accurate. This personal data is called "metadata" and is required in all files in order for your computer to index and find it quickly during a search. In this tip, we'll see how to view and erase metadata.

Additionally, you can remove other types of elements such as comments, track changes, and hidden content. Here is a full list of the types of things you can inspect for and remove instantly from your documents, spreadsheets and presentations.

Inspect For and Remove	Word	Excel	PowerPoint
Comments, Revisions, Versions, Annotations	X	X	X
Document Properties and Personal Information	X	X	X
Task Pane Apps	X	X	X

Inspect For and Remove	Word	Excel	PowerPoint
Content Apps		X	X
Collapsed Headings	X		
Custom XLM Data	X	X	X
Headers, Footers	X	X	
Watermarks	X		
Invisible Content	X	X	
Invisible On-Slide Content			X
Off-Slide Content			X
Hidden Text	X		
Hidden Rows and Columns		X	
Hidden Worksheets			
Data Model			

First, let's begin by reviewing the metadata contained in the document's properties and then walk through the steps to instantly erase that data before sending it to a customer or potential employer, or adversary.

To view personal data

1. Click the **File** tab to launch Backstage view. By default, this displays the **Info** section.
2. On the right side of the **Info** section is a list of properties about the document (as seen in Figure 18). This is the document's Metatdata.
3. To view more properties, click the **Show All Properties** link at the bottom of the list of properties.

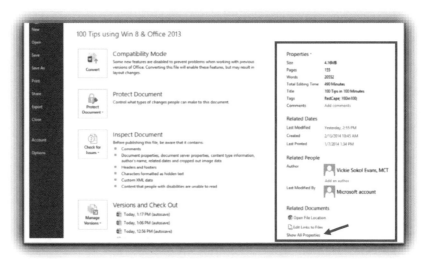

Figure 18. Backstage View: document properties

To avoid the risk of sharing personal or document information (which may or may not be accurate), you may want to remove the metadata from the file before sending the document to someone.

To remove your personal data

1. Click the **File** tab to get Backstage again and to display the **Info** section.
2. Click the **Check for Issues** button in the middle of the **Backstage** view and choose **Inspect Document** to launch the Document Inspector as seen in Figure 19.
3. Click **Inspect** to view all the metadata found in the document.
4. Click **Remove All** for **Document Properties and Personal Info**.

Figure 19. Document Inspector for Word

 To remove personal data in Office 2007, click the Office button and choose **Prepare**. Then click **Inspect Document**.

Tip #28 Mark a document as final

Applies to Office 2007, Office 2010, Office 2013

Once you have completed editing your document, spreadsheet or presentation – which, by the way, probably looks amazing if you've followed all these tips in this guide – you can specify that this file is the "Final Version". This will eliminate any confusion for you and others if there are multiple copies being emailed back and forth.

The good news is that Mark as Final isn't final. Mark as Final is a toggle feature under the Permissions section of Backstage as seen in Figure 20. It can be turned on and off as many times as you want, as you make those last minute changes. In order to make another change to the document, you must turn off Mark as Final, make your edits and then turn it back on.

Hey, maybe this would be a good button to add to your Quick Access Toolbar!

To mark a document as final

1. Click the **File** tab to view the **Info** section.
2. Click the **Protect Document** button in the middle of **Backstage** view.
3. Click **Mark as Final**.

Figure 20. Backstage View: Mark as Final

To make an edit to a document that is marked as final, repeat the steps above to turn it off. Once you make the necessary changes, turn **Mark as Final** back on.

To mark a document as final in Office 2007, click the Office button and choose **Prepare**. Then click **Mark as Final**.

 This tip meets the "Sharing and Maintaining Documents" objective of the Microsoft® Office Specialist exams for Word, Excel®, and PowerPoint®.

Word 2013

Save hours of formatting time.

Tip #29 Discover selecting tricks using the document margin

Applies to Word 2007, Word 2010, Word 2013

What happens when you move your mouse to the left margin? Did it turn into a white arrow pointing to the right as in Figure 21? The arrow shape actually has a purpose, believe it or not. The purpose of this arrow is to quickly select text with precision.

Figure 21. Selection arrow

To use the selection arrow

1. Move your mouse to the left-hand margin next to the text you wish to select.
2. Then perform the following actions:

Selection Arrow	Action
Single-click	Selects one line of text
Double-click	Selects one paragraph
Triple-click	Selects entire document

Tip #30 Use Styles to format your document

Applies to Word 2007, Word 2010, Word 2013

When working in long documents or repeatedly in short documents, you can save yourself considerable amount of time by using styles. Styles are saved formatting instructions that you can apply to a selection or entire paragraph. Not only do Styles save you formatting time, but it also creates a consistent and branded look for your document and makes updating the document a breeze. Styles also reduce formatting errors, which can prevent hours (and stress) of troubleshooting later.

To apply a Title style

1. Click in the paragraph that contains the title of the document.
2. On the **Home** tab, in the **Styles** group, click the style called **Title** as seen in Figure 22.

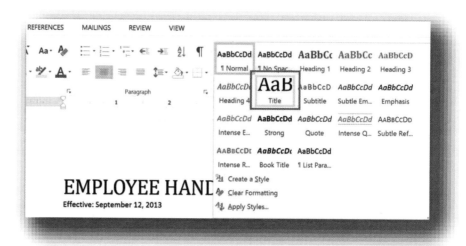

Figure 22. Apply the Title Style to the title of the document.

Note: If you do not see the Title style in the Styles gallery, click the **More** button on the side of the Styles window to display more styles as seen in Figure 23.

Figure 23. Styles Gallery "More" button

To apply styles to your headings

1. Click in one of your main heading paragraphs.
2. On the **Home** tab, in the **Styles** group, click the Quick Style called **Heading 1**.
3. If this main heading has a following subheading, click in the first subheading.
4. On the **Home** tab, in the **Styles** group, click the Quick Style called **Heading 2**.
5. Repeat as necessary, using the Headings 1-6 to establish your document hierarchy.

Your heading levels correspond with the hierarchy of your document headings, sub headings, sub sub-headings and so on -- similar to an outline.

This tip meets the "Formatting Content" objective of the Microsoft® Office Specialist exams for Word.

Tip #31 Use F4 to repeat last action

Applies to Word 2007, Word 2010, Word 2013

When you need to repeat the very last action in Word, you can use the keyboard shortcut [F4]. For instance, in the previous tip, you applied Heading 2 style to one of your sub headings. If you want to continue applying Heading 2 for the remainder of your level 2 headings in your document, you can scroll through your document and use the [F4] keyboard shortcut to apply the Heading 2 style.

To repeat the last action

1. After making a change to text, such as applying a heading style, navigate to the next heading that needs the same style you just applied.
2. Press [F4].
3. Navigate to the next heading that needs the same style and press [F4].
4. Repeat for the remainder of the document.

 [F4] only repeats the very last action. For example, if you applied a heading style, and then deleted some text in a paragraph below it, only the delete action would repeat, as this was the last action taken.

Tip #32 Select all text with similar formatting

Applies to Word 2007, Word 2010, Word 2013

When working in long documents or documents with a variety of formatting that must be consistent, such as a resume, you need a way to select all similarly formatted text throughout the entire document. Use the timesaving feature **Select all text with similar formatting** so that you can effortlessly:

- format the selected text a different way;
- copy and paste the content to another location or to another document; or
- delete content

To select all text with similar formatting

1. Click in the paragraph you want to use as your sample paragraph.

2. On the **Home** tab, in the **Editing** group, click **Select** to launch the Select menu as shown in Figure 24.
3. Click **Select All Text With Similar Formatting**.
4. Apply any new formats to the selected text in your document.

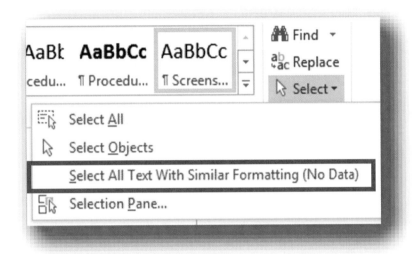

Figure 24. Select All Text With Similar Formatting (No Data)

Tip #33 Reformat your document in seconds

Applies to Word 2007, Word 2010, Word 2013

When you apply the standard Title and Heading styles to your document, your document takes on the format of the default Styles in Word. If you don't like the way your document looks after you've styled it, never fear! Style Sets are here!!

Style Sets are a collection of styles that can be used to instantly change the look of your document so that you're using the best format for that document type.

In the previous example, we styled our document using the default Title and Headings. Now let's completely restructure the document by changing the Style Set.

To use a Style Set to restructure your document

1. Click the **Design** tab.

2. Mouse over any of the Style Sets in the list to preview the changes to the document. Once you find one that works, simply click to choose it.

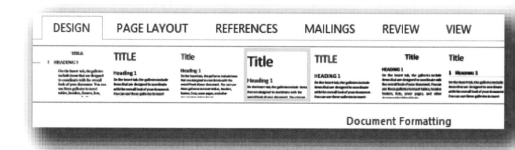

Figure 25. Change Style Set

You can always revert back to the default Style Set by choosing **Word 2013** from the Style Set list.

For Office 2007 and Office 2010, on the **Home** tab, in the **Styles** group, click the **Change Styles** button.

This tip meets the "Formatting Content" objective of the Microsoft® Office Specialist exams for Word.

Tip #34 Modify a style

Applies to Word 2007, Word 2010, Word 2013

One of the many ways to modify a style is to right-click the style name and select the option to modify it. This is called, modify by definition.

To modify a style by definition

1. On the **Home** tab, in the **Styles** group, right-click the style you wish to modify in the Quick Styles gallery.
2. Choose **Modify...** to open the Modify Style dialog box as seen in Figure 26.
3. Use the tools in the Formatting section of the dialog box to edit the style, or click the **Format** dropdown button at the bottom left-hand corner of the dialog box to see more formatting options.

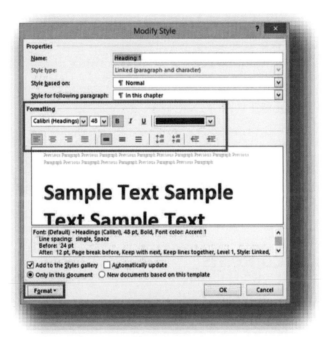

Figure 26. Modify Style dialog box

This tip meets the "Formatting Content" objective of the Microsoft® Office Specialist exams for Word.

Tip #35 Create a table of contents in seconds

Applies to Word 2007, Word 2010, Word 2013

There are a couple of ways you can create a table of contents (also known as TOC). You can either mark entries in your document that you want displayed in your TOC or you can tell Word to generate the TOC from your styles.

Since you have already styled your document (see Tip #30), the easiest way to create a table of contents is to use the built-in heading styles or any custom styles you have created and applied. The procedure below assumes you formatted a document by using heading styles.

Create a table of contents from built-in heading styles

1. Click where you want to insert the table of contents, usually at the beginning of a document.
2. On the **References** tab, in the **Table of Contents** group, click **Table of Contents**, and then click the Automatic Table 1 style or the Automatic Table 2 style as seen in Figure 27.

Figure 27. Table of Contents menu on the ribbon

To customize your Table of Contents

1. Click somewhere in your TOC.
2. Click the **References** tab.

3. In the **Table of Contents** group, click the **Table of Contents** dropdown arrow and choose **Customize Table of Contents** to open the Table of Contents window.

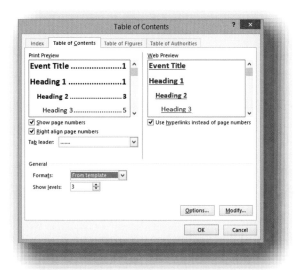

Figure 28. Table of Contents window

4. Configure the following settings for your TOC:
5. Show page number (ON by default)
6. Right align page numbers (ON by default)
7. Tab leader (set to dotted tab leader by default)
8. Formats (choose your favorite)
9. Show Levels (set how many heading levels you want)
10. Options – select the Options button if you need to select additional styles to bring into your TOC
11. Click **Ok**.

On the **References** tab, in the **Table of Contents** group, click **Insert Table of Contents** to launch the Table of Contents window.

 This tip meets the "Applying References and Hyperlinks" objective of the Microsoft® Office Specialist exams for Word.

Tip #36 Create a professional cover page in an instant

Applies to Word 2007, Word 2010, Word 2013

When creating a title page or cover page for your document, you can eliminate the time consuming process of inserting a blank page, adding your title, subtitle, company info, lots of blank lines to position the content, and section breaks to control the page numbering. You can even eliminate the time it takes to format all the various elements of your cover page. You can do this by inserting one of Word's professionally designed cover pages.

Create a professional cover page in an instant

1. You don't have to worry about where your cursor is since Cover Pages are always added to the beginning of your document. On the **Insert** tab, in the **Pages** group, click the **Cover Page** drop down.
2. Scroll through the gallery of cover pages to select the one you want. Word will insert your new cover page at the beginning of the document.
3. Using the document controls to guide you, enter the applicable Title, Subtitle, Author, etc. in the cover page.
4. To change to a different cover page, repeat steps 1 and 2 above. There is no need to remove the original cover page.

Tip #37 Format a table in seconds

Applies to Word 2007, Word 2010, Word 2013

Not only can you instantly format text using styles, you can do the same for your tables using Table styles. When you click inside a table, you will see the Table Tools contextual tabs appear on the Ribbon as seen in Figure 29. If you do not see these tabs, you have not clicked inside a table.

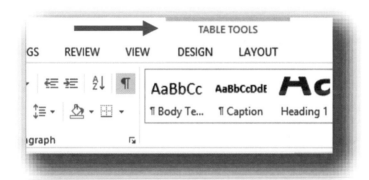

Figure 29. Table Tools contextual tabs on the Ribbon

To format your table using a table style

1. Click in your table or select it so that you see the Table Tools contextual tabs on the ribbon.
2. On the **Table Tools Design** tab, in the **Table Styles** group, click the **More** button (as seen in Figure 30) to expand the list of Table Styles.
3. Mouse over any of the sample styles to see what it will look like in your document.
4. Click the style you wish to apply.

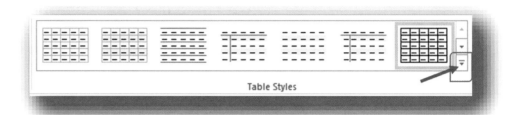

Figure 30. The Table Styles "More" button on the Table Design ribbon

This tip meets the "Formatting Content" objective of the Microsoft® Office Specialist exams for Word.

Tip #38 Effortlessly move table rows

Applies to Word 2007, Word 2010, Word 2013

Your table looks amazing (after Tip #36) but you notice a slight problem. You realize that you need to move content from one row, above another row. Rather than insert a row and retype the info, you can use a powerful keyboard shortcut.

To effortlessly move table rows

1. Click in the row that needs to be moved.
2. Press [Shift]+[Alt]+Up Arrow (or Down Arrow) to move the row to the right spot.

Tip #39 Confidently delete a table

Applies to Word 2007, Word 2010, Word 2013

When you want to delete your table, it is common to select the entire table and then press the [DELETE] key on your keyboard. Unfortunately, that deletes only the text.

To delete the entire table, including the text

- Select the table and use the [BACKSPACE] key instead of the [DELETE] key.

Tip #40 Use your headings to navigate your document

Applies to Word 2007, Word 2010, Word 2013

Once you have styles applied to your headings and subheadings, you can use those headings to navigate quickly through your document by using Word's Navigation Pane.

To use the Navigation Pane to navigate your document

1. On the **View** tab, in the **Show** group, click the **Navigation Pane** check box. If you are using Styles for your headings and text, hooray! You will see your headings and subheadings in the Navigation Pane on the left side of your screen.
2. Click on any heading text in the Navigation Pane to jump to that section in the document.

Note: If you do not see anything in the Navigation Pane after step #1 above, that means the document isn't formatted using Heading styles. Go back to Tip #30 and apply your Heading styles to your main headings and subheadings.

New in 2013, collapse and expand your headings right in your document! Each of your Heading paragraphs – those where you have applied a heading style – will have a triangle in the left margin when you click in the paragraph. Click to collapse that parent heading to temporarily hide its subheadings, or what I like to call them. "baby" headings.

To use your headings to navigate your document in Word 2007, on the **View** tab, in the **Show** group, click **Document Map**.

Tip #41 Easily move content like never before

Applies to Word 2010, Word 2013

It is now easier than ever to move blocks of content to another location in your document by using the Navigation Pane. This is a great way to change the order of content within your document rather than using cut and paste or drag and drop, both of which can be risky. When you move headings in your navigation pane, the corresponding subheadings (if any) and body text, tables, and other objects will move with it.

To move content using the Navigation Pane

1. Display your Navigation Pane: On the **View** tab, in the **Show** group, click the **Navigation Pane** check box. If you are using Styles for your headings and text, hooray! You will see your headings and subheadings in the Navigation Pane on the left side of your screen.
2. In the Navigation Pane, drag the heading you want to move above or below another heading in the document.

As seen in Figure 31, you can also right-click any heading to perform additional actions such as:

- Promoting or demoting a heading.
- Adding a new heading before or after the current heading.
- Adding a subheading.
- Deleting a heading.
- Select Heading and Content
- Print heading and content
- Expand and collapse headings
- Specify which heading levels to view

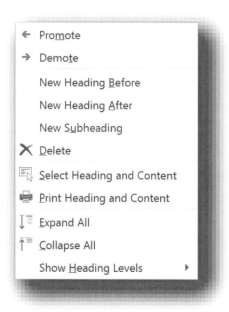

Figure 31. Navigation Pane Right-Click Menu

 Note: If you do not see anything in the Navigation Pane after step #1 above, that means the document isn't formatted using styles. Go back to Tip #30.

Tip #42 Use keyboard shortcuts to navigate your document

Applies to Word 2007, Word 2010, Word 2013

Use these universal keyboard shortcuts to help you get around you document faster than ever before. All four of these shortcuts apply to most Microsoft Office programs as well as other technologies.

To go to the top of your document

▨ Use the [CTRL]+[HOME] keyboard shortcut.

To go to the end of your document

▨ Use the [CTRL]+[END] keyboard shortcut.

To go to the beginning of a line

- Use the [HOME] keyboard shortcut.

To go to the end of the line

- Use the [END] keyboard shortcut.

Excel 2013

Save time in Excel using "back to basics" tools.

Tip #43 Use Autofill to save time and reduce errors

Applies to Excel 2007, Excel 2010, Excel 2013

When working with time dimensions such as days, weeks, months, quarters and time of day, you can count on Excel to do much of the work for you when it comes to typing the data into your sheet. After typing one month or day of the week, use a feature called Autofill to fill in the pattern and complete the list. For instance, suppose you need the months "Jan" through "Dec" across your sheet as column headers, type the first month and then use Autofill to complete the remaining months.

To Autofill months in your sheet

1. Type the name of a month in a cell. Type either the full month or the abbreviated 3-character version, such as Jan for January, and press [ENTER].
2. Position your mouse over the AutoFill handle located in the bottom right-hand corner of your selected cell. Your mouse pointer should be a black plus sign.
3. Drag the black plus sign either down or to the right to Autofill the remaining values.

You can also use this trick for Quarters, Days of the Week and more! See Table 1 on page 65 for a list of series you can fill using the Autofill feature.

Autofill to create a schedule of 30 minute increments

Autofill also works with date and time. But there's one extra little step when working with dates and time because Excel doesn't know what increment you want. If you Autofill a date, such as today's date, Excel will assume you want the next value to be one day later and the series will Autofill by increments of a day. But what if you wanted to increase by weeks instead of days?

Likewise, when you Autofill a time, such as 8:00 AM, Excel gives you the next hour, 9:00AM. What if you wanted 30 minute increments instead of hour increments? The trick is to tell Excel exactly what number sequence you want by typing in the first two values and THEN using Autofill with both of those values to complete the series.

Create a schedule in 30 minute increments

1. In the first cell, type 8:00 AM, or whatever start time increment you need, press [ENTER].
2. In the second cell, type 8:30 AM, or thirty minutes from the previous time you typed, press [ENTER].
3. Select both cells, (make sure your mouse is in the shape of a big white plus sign).
4. Mouse over the Autofill handle, located in the bottom right-hand corner of your selected cells. Your mouse will turn into the shape of a small, black plus sign.
5. Drag down or across as needed.

Use Autofill to copy calculations

Not only can you use Autofill to copy time dimensions as we saw in the previous step, but we can use it to copy calculations. In Figure 32, the Total calculation for Dallas sales has been entered and is selected. Rather than type the calculation in each of the other locations or copy and paste the calculation, you can use Autofill instead to save even more time.

1. Create the calculation in the first cell of your series.
2. Use the Autofill handle located in the bottom right-hand corner of your selected cell to drag down a column or across a row.

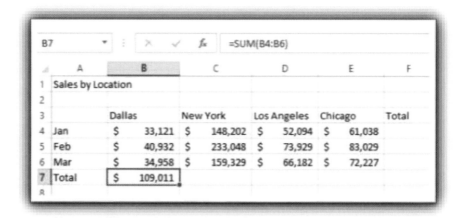

Figure 32. Copy total calculation using Autofill

Instantly Autofill down a column

Now that you have had a little practice using Autofill to enter time dimensions in different increments and to copy calculations, it is time to learn yet another timesaving shortcut using Autofill. Rather than drag the Autofill handle, you can double-click the Autofill handle to fill the series for you.

1. Select the cell you wish to Autofill down your list of data.
2. Position your mouse pointer on the Autofill handle (the bottom right-hand corner of the cell).
3. When your mouse pointer turns into a black plus sign double-click the Autofill handle, and the data is instantly added down the column.

Note: for the Autofill handle to operate instantly down the column, there must be a data column to the left or right; otherwise the double-click option will not work and you will need to drag the mouse down instead.

Examples of series that you can fill

Initial selection	Extended series
1, 2, 3	4, 5, 6,...
9:00	10:00, 11:00, 12:00,...
Mon	Tue, Wed, Thu,...
Monday	Tuesday, Wednesday, Thursday,...
Jan	Feb, Mar, Apr,...
Jan, Apr	Jul, Oct, Jan,...
Jan-07, Apr-07	Jul-07, Oct-07, Jan-08,...
15-Jan, 15-Apr	15-Jul, 15-Oct,...
2007, 2008	2009, 2010, 2011,...
1-Jan, 1-Mar	1-May, 1-Jul, 1-Sep,...
Qtr3 (or Q3 or Quarter3)	Qtr4, Qtr1, Qtr2,...
text1, textA	text2, textA, text3, textA,...
1st Period	2nd Period, 3rd Period,...
Product 1	Product 2, Product 3,...

Table 1 Examples of Autofill series

Tip #44 Quickly select a table in Excel

Applies to Excel 2007, Excel 2010, Excel 2013

To quickly select a table

1. Click any cell within your table.
2. Use the [Ctrl]+[A] keyboard shortcut.

To select your entire worksheet, do one of the following

1. Click in a cell that isn't a part of a list and use the [Ctrl]+[A] keyboard shortcut.
   OR
2. Click the empty header tab to the left of Column A and above Row 1 as seen in Figure 33.

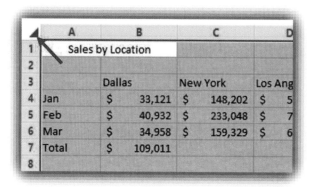

Figure 33. The Select All button

Tip #45 Use Excel's AutoFit to resize columns and rows

Applies to Excel 2007, Excel 2010, Excel 2013

It is inevitable that the standard column width of 8.43 is too narrow to display all the contents in your columns. You can easily resize a column either with the mouse or by right-clicking and choosing Column Width. But what if you have multiple columns that need to be resized? What if the rows need to be resized as well? You certainly don't want to have to visit every single column and every single row to manually resize them. Instead, use a feature called AutoFit.

To resize one column using AutoFit

1. Position your cursor at the right-most edge of the column header so that your mouse turns into a double-headed arrow. For instance, if you want to resize column A, hover your mouse in between column A and column B to get the double-headed arrow.
2. Next, double-click on the vertical line that separates the two columns. Excel will automatically resize the left column to the width of the cell that has the longest value.

To resize one row using AutoFit

▪ Autofit works for rows, too! When you double-click the horizontal line between two rows, Excel will apply the Best Fit to the row above the horizontal line.

To resize all columns and all rows using AutoFit

1. Click the Select All button in the upper left-hand corner of your worksheet, to the left of the A column and above row 1. See Figure 33.
2. Mouse over the line between two columns to get the double-headed arrow and then double-click the vertical line that separates the columns.
3. Next, mouse over the line between two rows to get the double-headed arrow and then double-click the horizontal line that separates the rows. This method gives you the best fit for all columns and rows in your document.

Tip #46 Open another instance of Excel automatically

Applies to Excel 2007, Excel 2010, Excel 2013

One of the most popular Excel questions is how to open up multiple instances of Excel so that you can toggle between two Excel windows using [Alt]+[Tab] or so that you can view the workbooks side by side either on one monitor or on two.

New in Excel 2013, files by default now open in separate instances (or windows) so you can view them side by side or toggle nicely between every Excel file you open. So you don't have to do a thing!

To open multiple instances of Excel

1. Launch Excel.
2. Open one file.
3. Open a second file.
4. Then move the second file to another monitor, or use your Windows + left or Windows + right arrow to snap the windows side by side as mentioned in "View windows side by side" for 0 on page 4.

You now are able to copy and/or move worksheets in between workbooks even if they are open in separate instances of Excel! We weren't able to do that with separate windows before. Hooray!!

In Excel 2010 or earlier, you can't natively toggle or view two Excel files side by side on multiple monitors. Instead, you have a workaround. Once you have your first file open in Excel, you will see the Excel icon in the Taskbar. Right-click the Excel icon in the Taskbar and select Microsoft Excel 2010 and it will open a new instance of Excel. Then you must open your 2nd Excel file by using **File** > **Open**.

Manage your data with minimal effort.

One of the most valuable and time saving features first introduced in Excel 2007, is Format as a Table. The benefits of formatting your list as a table include:

- Filters are included
- Remove duplicates easily
- Instantly format the table
- Add a total row using a toggle button
- Create calculated columns
- View table headings when you scroll
- Easily rearrange columns
- Easily select columns
- New columns and rows are automatically added to the defined table range
- Delete rows in your table without affecting surrounding rows in other tables
- You can name your table to keep your data organized, to use as a shortcut and to use as a reference for PivotTables and Charts

As you can see, there are numerous benefits to formatting your list as a table but there are also a few limitations. You will need to convert your table back to a range by clicking the **Convert to Range** button on the **Table Tools** tab in the **Tools** group if you want to do the following:

- Use the Subtotals feature
- Transpose the data

Tip #47 Format a list as a Table

Applies to Excel 2007, Excel 2010, Excel 2013

Before you can reap the many benefits of a table, you must first format your list as a table.

To format your list as a table

1. Select the range of data in your list you wish to format as a table or click in any cell of your table and press [Ctrl]+[A], which should select

your entire table as long as you do not have any empty rows or columns.

2. On the **Home** tab, in the **Styles** group, click the **Format As Table** button to launch the table styles dropdown menu. Select the first one in the list to get started. You can always change it later.

3. Make sure the range of data you want to format as a list is correct and that it has the correct setting for **My table has headers**. Then click **Ok**.

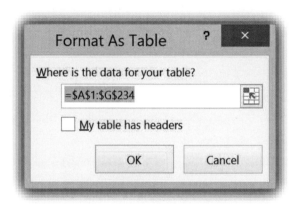

Figure 34. Format as Table dialog box

Tip #48 Sort and use Autofilter to find data

Applies to Excel 2007, Excel 2010, Excel 2013

Filtering allows you to easily find and work with a subset of records in your table. It shows the records that meet your criteria and hide the records that do not. You can even filter on multiple columns.

When you format your list as a table, filter buttons are automatically added to the header row saving you time from having to insert them yourself.

To find data using Autofilter

1. With your data formatted as a table from the previous step, click one of the dropdown arrows of a column in your header row.

2. Use any one or a combination of filters to find your data.

A quicker way to filter is typing the criteria for the filter in the search box rather than scrolling through a long list of values.

Tip #49 Use the new Slicer feature to filter your table easier than ever

New in Excel 2013

My students tell me that their favorite new Table feature is the Slicer! Slicers were introduced in Excel 2010, but they were only available for PivotTables as a way to easily filter our reports, with style and control.

To add Slicers to your table for easy filtering

1. Click anywhere in your table to activate the **Table Tools Design** tab on the ribbon.
2. In the **Tools** group, click **Insert Slicer** to display a list of fields available from your table.
3. Click any of the fields that you plan to use to filter your data. You can pick as many as you like. But two or three is a good start.
4. Click **Ok** to view the two or three slicer boxes.
5. You can move the slicers anywhere on your worksheet and resize them.
6. Use the slicers (one or all of them) to filter you data like magic. To unfilter, click the red X on the specific slicer.

Tip: I like my to position my slicers in either in row 1 or column A so that even if new rows or columns are added, my slicers don't get in the way. You can always resize row 1 and column A to fit your slicers, or vice versa.

Be sure to check out the **Slicer Tools Options** tab in the ribbon to see how you can customize your Slicers to be different colors, multiple columns, etc. Who knew reporting in Excel could be this fun!?!

71

Tip #50 Expand the table as you type

Applies to Excel 2007, Excel 2010, Excel 2013

Once your list is formatted as a table, you can use many of the features of an Excel table, such as Table AutoExpansion. As you add text to a column or row next to a table, Excel will automatically include that column or row in the table. In most cases, this is extremely convenient and when it is not, you always have the ability to stop expanding.

To expand the table as you type

▪ Start typing content in the first column that is not part of your table. As soon as you press [ENTER] or [TAB] or click out of the cell, Excel adds that new column to the defined table.

To decline Table AutoExpansion

▪ As soon as Excel expands the table to include the new column or row, you will see the AutoCorrect Options Tag next to your column as seen in Figure 35. Click the Options Tag and select Stop Automatically Expanding Tables and the new data you typed will not be included with the table.

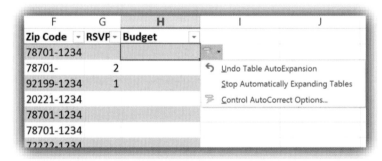

Figure 35. AutoCorrect Options Tag for Automatically Expanding Tables

To turn off AutoExpansion altogether

1. Click the Options Tag as seen in Figure 35. The AutoCorrect dialog box opens.
2. On the **AutoFormat As You Type** tab select **Control AutoCorrect Options...**
3. Uncheck the second option "Include new rows and columns in the table" as seen in Figure 36 and click **Ok**.

Figure 36. AutoCorrect Dialog Box to stop auto-expanding tables

Changing this option will turn off Table AutoExpansion in the workbook and in any workbook you have open in this instance of Excel. If you open another instance of Excel, Table AutoExpansion is on by default. To open another instance of Excel, see Tip #46.

To return to the AutoFormat As You Type setting, on to the **File** tab, click **Options**. Click on the **Proofing** category on the left and click **AutoCorrect Options….** Make sure the AutoFormat As You Type tab is selected.

Tip #51 Create a calculated column with minimal effort
Applies to Excel 2007, Excel 2010, Excel 2013

With your data in a table, you can create a calculation in any cell and Excel will automatically copy that calculation to every cell in that column within the table without missing a beat. When necessary, you still have the option to stop the Calculated Column feature.

Note: this does not work unless your list is formatted as a table.

To create a calculated column in your table

1. Click in any cell of the column you wish to add the calculation.
2. Add the calculation in that cell by creating a formula or function and click [ENTER] or [TAB]. Every cell in that column should now have the calculation you just created.

To decline Calculated Column

▪ As soon as Excel adds the calculation to every cell in the column, you will see the AutoCorrect Options Tag next to your column as seen in Figure 37. Click the Options Tag and select **Stop Automatically Creating Calculated Columns**. The new calculation you typed will only apply to the current cell and will not be added to every cell in that column.

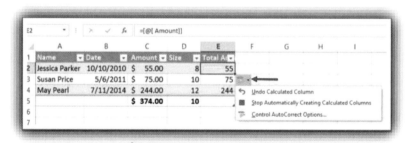

Figure 37. AutoCorrect Options Tab for Calculated Columns

To turn off Calculated Columns altogether (not recommended)

1. Click the **Options** Tag as seen in Figure 37 and on the AutoFormat As You Type tab select **Control AutoCorrect Options…**
2. In the AutoCorrect dialog box as seen in Figure 38, uncheck the third option "Fill formulas in tables to create calculated columns" and click **Ok**.

Figure 38. AutoCorrect Dialog Box to stop creating calculated columns

Changing this option will turn off the Calculated Columns in the current workbook and in any workbook you also have open in this instance of Excel. If you open another instance of Excel, Calculated Columns is on by default. To open another instance of Excel, see Tip #46.

To return to the AutoFormat As You Type setting, on to the **File** tab, click **Options**. Click on the **Proofing** category on the left and click **AutoCorrect Options….** Make sure the AutoFormat As You Type tab is selected.

Tip #52 Instantly add a total row to your table

Applies to Excel 2007, Excel 2010, Excel 2013

When you're ready to add a row at the bottom of your table to count rows in your table or sum a column, you can rely on your mouse clicking skills, not your math skills, to do all the work for you.

To add a total row to your table

1. With your list now formatted as a table, click anywhere in the table to activate the **Table Tools** contextual tabs.

2. On the **Design** tab, in the **Table Style Options** group, click the **Total Row** option.
3. Click in any cell within your new total row and click the dropdown arrow to select the function to apply in that column.
4. To turn off the total row, click the **Design** tab, and in the **Table Style Options** group and uncheck the **Total Row** option.

Tip #53 Add style to your table

Applies to Excel 2007, Excel 2010, Excel 2013

You do not have to be a graphic designer or have an eye for color to turn your table of data into a professional and eye catching report that people will actually read. Let Excel do all the work for you using table styles and to save even more time, rely on gallery previews in Excel 2013 to show you what the table will look like before you apply the style.

To add style to your table

1. With your list formatted as a table, click inside your table so that the **Table Tools** contextual tab is displayed.
2. On the **Design** tab, in the **Table Styles** group, mouse over any one of the Table Styles to preview a table style.
3. Click the **More** button on the ribbon, as seen in Figure 39, to display more table style formats.

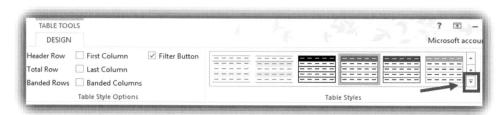

Figure 39. Table Styles More button

4. When you find the one you like, simply click on the style to apply.

In Office 2007, when you hover over a table style it does not show a preview of the table style first as described in step 2. Instead, you must click on one of the styles to view the table style applied to your table.

Tip #54 Select all cells in a column with ease

Applies to Excel 2007, Excel 2010, Excel 2013

Selecting a range of cells can certainly be tricky at times, especially if it involves scrolling to get to the end of the range. Never fear, use this one click method to select all the cells within one column and nothing more (or less).

To select all cells in a column with ease

1. With your list formatted as a table, select the first cell in your column that you want to select as a whole. The first cell should be the name of your column.
2. Position your mouse on the border of that selected column name and your mouse should turn into a four-headed arrow.
3. With your mouse in the shape of the four-headed arrow, click the border of the column name and that will select the column in that table and no other rows outside the table.

Tip #55 Remove duplicate records

Applies to Excel 2007, Excel 2010, Excel 2013

When you're worried about having duplicate records in your list, you no longer have to waste any time or risk having an inaccurate list. With you list formatted as a table, you can easily remove duplicates with in just a couple of clicks!

To remove duplicate records in your table

1. With your list formatted as a table, click inside your table so that the **Table Tools** contextual tab is displayed.
2. On the **Design** tab, in the **Tools** group, click the **Remove Duplicates** option as shown in Figure 40 to launch the **Remove Duplicates** dialog box

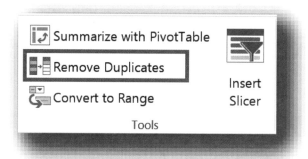

Figure 40. Remove Duplicates command on the Ribbon

3. If you want Excel to look for duplicate rows by evaluating the data in every column, click **Ok**. Otherwise, use the checkboxes to identify which columns Excel should examine for duplicates.

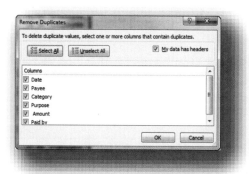

Figure 41. Remove Duplicates dialog box

4. In the **Remove Duplicates** window, as seen in Figure 41, uncheck the columns you wish not to look for duplicates and click **OK**.

5. When Excel has finished, a results window displays telling you how many duplicates it found and how many unique values remain in your table.

Figure 42 Delete Duplicates Results Window

Save time and reduce errors using magical tools.

Tip #56 Use Autocalculate to show off your math skills

Applies to Excel 2007, Excel 2010, Excel 2013

When you need to calculate a range of cells quickly in Excel, you no longer need to create the calculation yourself. It is just a matter of looking at your status bar.

To quickly calculate a range of cells

1. Select the range of cells on your worksheet you wish to calculate.
2. Look at your status bar at the bottom of the worksheet to view the Count, Average and Total as shown in Figure 43.

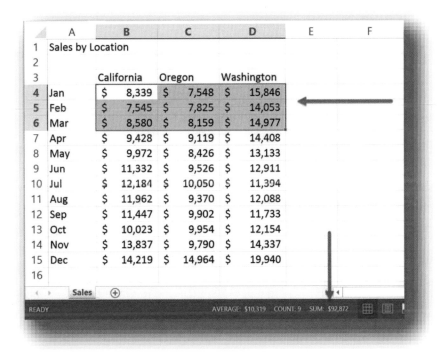

Figure 43 AutoCalculate using the Status Bar

3. If you wish to see more calculations, right-click the status bar to display the **Customize Status Bar** window as seen in Figure 43 and select more functions from the list of options.

✓	Average	$10,319
✓	Count	9
	Numerical Count	
	Minimum	
	Maximum	
✓	Sum	$92,872

Figure 44. AutoCalculate right-click menu on the Status Bar

Tip #57 Separate a Full Name column into First and Last Name columns

Applies to Excel 2007, Excel 2010, Excel 2013

When you need to separate data within a cell into multiple cells you can use the Text to Columns button on the Data tab. For example, you can separate one column with full names of customers into multiple columns that separate the first name from the last name.

To separate full names into first name and last name

1. Make sure you have several empty columns to the right of your Full name column so that Excel has a place to store the newly separated values. You may need to insert two or three new columns.
2. Select the Full Name column. Again, make sure there are empty columns to the right of the Full Name column.
3. From the **Data** tab, in the **Data Tools** group, select **Text To Columns** to launch the **Convert Text to Columns Wizard**.
4. In Step 1 of the wizard as seen in Figure 45, choose **Delimited** and click **Next**.

Figure 45. Convert Text to Columns Wizard - Step 1 of 3: Select Delimited

5. In Step 2 of the wizard as seen in Figure 46, select which type of delimiter (or separator) the data has. When finished, click **Next**.

Figure 46. Convert to Text Columns Wizard - Step 2 of 3: Choose your delimiter

6. In Step 3 as seen in Figure 47, accept the default **General** setting for **Column data format** for text values, date values and any numeric values. However, if your column is a zip code or phone number

column – a column that stores numbers that will never be used in a calculation – then you'll want to be sure you select each of the General columns in the Preview area of this window and change them to Text. Do that for each General column you see in your window. Other

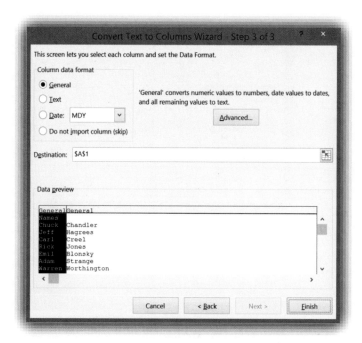

Figure 47. Convert Text to Columns Wizard - Step 3 of 3: Confirm data type and format

7. Click **Finish**.

Tip #58 Use the new Flash Fill feature to create new columns of data

New in Excel 2013

My most favorite feature introduced in Excel 2013, is Flash Fill. I get goose bumps EVERY TIME I use it.

Suppose you want to create a new column in your data called Full Name. You have the first name in one column and the last name in another column. Flash fill will recognize the pattern after the first few combinations and will complete the pattern for you. Love, love, love!

Combining multiple columns has never been easier. Check it out!

To use Flash Fill to create a Full Name column

1. Assuming you have a column of first names and a column of last names (in two separate columns) create a new column called "Full Name".
2. In the first cell, start typing the full name based on the values in the First Name and Last Name column in that row.
3. In the second cell, type the full name for this person based on the values in the First Name and Last Name column in that row.
4. In the third cell, start typing the Full Name and notice that Excel begins to understand that you're taking the First and Last names and combining them.
5. Click [Enter] to confirm the Flash Fill prediction and BAM, you're done!
6. This works for just about many other types of data clean up.
7. Try it out for the Last,First column. Type the last name, then a comma, then a space and then the first name for the first two people. BAM… Flash Fill should complete the rest. #goosebumps

Tip #59 Paste values instead of formulas

Applies to Excel 2007, Excel 2010, Excel 2013

You can copy and paste formulas throughout your spreadsheet but what if you want Excel to copy and paste the formula's value rather than the formula itself? You can use a command called Paste Values.

To paste values instead of formulas

1. Select the cells that contain the values you want.
2. On the **Home** tab, in the **Clipboard** group, click **Copy**.
3. Select the destination cell.
4. On the **Home** tab, in the **Clipboard** group, click the **Paste dropdown arrow** to view the dropdown menu as seen in Figure 48.

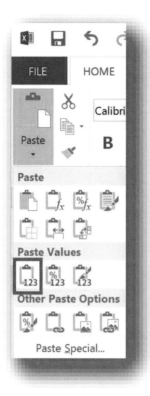

Figure 48. The Values button on the Paste dropdown menu

5. Under the **Paste Values** heading, click the icon called **Values**.

 You can also use the keyboard shortcut [CTRL]+[ALT]+[V] to launch the Paste Special dialog box. For instance, copy the cell contents, then click in your destination cell and press [CTRL]+[ALT]+[V]. Select **Values** and click [ENTER].

Tip #60 Flip your data using transpose text

Applies to Excel 2007, Excel 2010, Excel 2013

When you need to see your columns as rows and your rows as columns, you can easily flip the data using transpose text.

To transpose your text

1. Select the text or table you want to flip or transpose.
2. On the **Home** tab, in the **Clipboard** group, click **Copy**.
3. Select the upper left-hand cell of the paste area.

4. On the **Home** tab, in the **Clipboard** group, click the Paste dropdown arrow to view the dropdown menu as seen in Figure 49.

5. Under the **Paste** heading, click the last icon called **Transpose**.

Figure 49. The Transpose command on the Paste dropdown menu

 You can also use the keyboard shortcut [CTRL]+[ALT]+[V] to launch the Paste Special dialog box. For instance, copy the cell contents, then click in your destination cell and press [CTRL]+[ALT]+[V]. Select **Transpose** and click [ENTER].

Tip #61 Create a chart at the press of a button

Applies to Excel 2007, Excel 2010, Excel 2013

When working in Excel, there are many times when the hardest part is just getting started. The easiest way to get started with a chart is by using a keyboard shortcut.

To create a chart at the press of a button

1. Select the range you want to chart.
2. Press [F11] on your keyboard to launch a basic bar chart on a new worksheet.
3. Use the **Chart Tools** contextual tab on the Ribbon to modify your new chart.

New in Excel 2013, is the Quick Analysis tool that appears in the right-hand corner of the selected data as seen in Figure 50. Clicking this button allows you to create the chart you want in just a few clicks. See Tip #65 for more information.

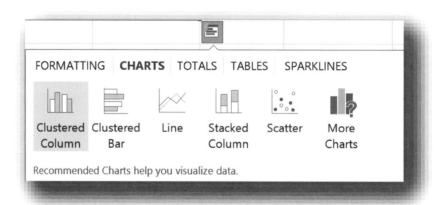

Figure 50. Quick Analysis Options > Charts Tab

Tip #62 Flag duplicate values in your column

Excel 2007, Excel 2010, Excel 2013

When you need to monitor your data for duplicates, Excel's conditional formatting will do the trick.

Suppose you have a list of potential customers that you are collecting from various events and you want to limit the list to unique customer email addresses. As you type in a new customer in your spreadsheet, you want Excel to flag the email you just entered if it is already in the list so that you can move on to the next unique customer entry.

To flag duplicate values

1. Select the column you wish check for duplicates.
2. On the **Home** tab, in the **Styles** group, click **Conditional Formatting**, which displays the **Conditional Formatting** dropdown menu.
3. Select **Highlight Cell Rules** and then choose **Duplicate Values...**, which displays the **Duplicate Values** dialog box as seen in Figure 51.

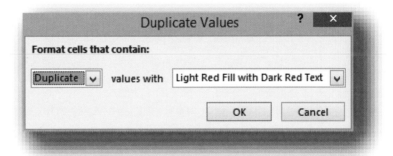

Figure 51. Duplicate Values dialog box

4. Accept the default setting or choose a different setting using the dropdown menus in the **Duplicate Values** dialog box and click **Ok**.

Tip #63 Find anomalies using a heat map

Applies to Excel 2007, Excel 2010, Excel 2013

One of the many ways you can see the story behind your data is to use conditional formatting, specifically a heat map. In this example, we will apply Color Scales conditional formatting to the columns of data that allowed us to find an anomaly or error in our data.

To create a heat map of your values

1. Select the columns you wish to evaluate.
2. On the **Home** tab, in the **Styles** group, click **Conditional Formatting**.

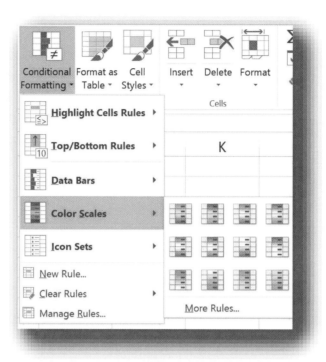

Figure 52. Insert a Heat Map using Color Scales

3. In the **Color Scales** category, mouse over each color scale option to see a preview of the heat map.
4. Select the Color Scales pattern you prefer and your report will look similar to a heat map as seen in Figure 53.

Sales by Location			
	California	Oregon	Washington
Jan	$ 8,339	$ 7,548	$ 15,846
Feb	$ 7,545	$ 7,825	$ 14,053
Mar	$ 8,580	$ 8,159	$ 14,977
Apr	$ 9,428	$ 9,119	$ 14,408
May	$ 9,972	$ 8,426	$ 13,133
Jun	$ 11,332	$ 9,526	$ 12,911
Jul	$ 12,184	$ 10,050	$ 11,394
Aug	$ 11,962	$ 9,370	$ 12,088
Sep	$ 11,447	$ 9,902	$ 11,733
Oct	$ 10,023	$ 9,954	$ 12,154
Nov	$ 13,837	$ 9,790	$ 14,337
Dec	$ 14,219	$ 14,964	$ 19,940

Figure 53. Heat Map of Sales Data

New in Excel 2013 is the Quick Analysis tool that appears in the right-hand corner of the selected data as seen in Figure 54. Clicking this button allows you to apply a color scale heat map to your data with two clicks. See Tip #65 for more information.

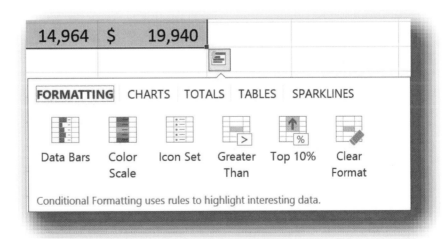

Figure 54. Quick Analysis Options > Formatting Tab

Tip #64 See the trend in each row using Sparklines

Applies to Excel 2010, Excel 2013

Sparklines are tiny charts that reside in a cell to show trends and the story behind your data quickly and easily. As you can see in Figure 55, Washington outdid the other two cities except in July when California was the high. Including the Sparklines in this report, makes it so much easier to see what happened over the year and how sales may trend in the coming year.

Sales by Location	California	Oregon	Washington	
Jan	$ 8,339	$ 7,548	$ 15,846	▬ ▬ ■
Feb	$ 7,545	$ 7,825	$ 14,053	▬ ▬ ■
Mar	$ 8,580	$ 8,159	$ 14,977	▬ ▬ ■
Apr	$ 9,428	$ 9,119	$ 14,408	▬ ▬ ■
May	$ 9,972	$ 8,426	$ 13,133	▬ ▬ ■
Jun	$ 11,332	$ 9,526	$ 12,911	▬ ▬ ■
Jul	$ 12,184	$ 10,050	$ 11,394	■ ▬ ▬
Aug	$ 11,962	$ 9,370	$ 12,088	■ ▬ ■
Sep	$ 11,447	$ 9,902	$ 11,733	■ ▬ ■
Oct	$ 10,023	$ 9,954	$ 12,154	▬ ▬ ■
Nov	$ 13,837	$ 9,790	$ 14,337	■ ▬ ■
Dec	$ 14,219	$ 14,964	$ 19,940	▬ ▬ ■

Figure 55. Example of a Sparkline report

To create a Sparkline chart

1. Select the first empty cell to the right of your range of data.
2. On the **Insert** tab, in the **Sparklines** group, click **Line**, **Bar** or **Win/Loss**.
3. Click in the Data box and highlight the range for which you want to view the trend. Hint: be sure not to include the final year-end total if you have one.
4. Click **Ok**.
5. Using the Autofill handle of the cell with the new Sparkline chart, copy the Sparkline down the other cells if necessary. See Tip #43 for help with Autofill.

New in Excel 2013 is the Quick Analysis tool that appears in the right-hand corner of the selected data as seen in Figure 56. Clicking this button allows you to select Sparklines for the entire list with two clicks. See Tip #65 for more information.

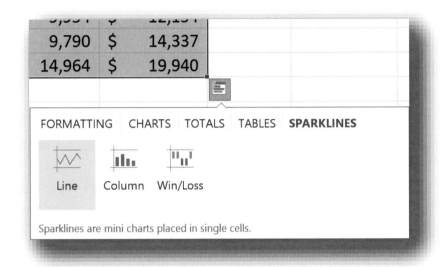

Figure 56. Quick Analysis Options > Sparklines

Tip #65 Use the new Quick Analysis Tool

New in Excel 2013

All data tells a story. How did we do last quarter? How is attendance tracking? Will we break even? Do we have enough widgets?

Now in Excel 2013, creating different types of charts and visuals to tell that story is easier than ever with the latest tool in Excel called Quick Analysis.

To activate the Quick Analysis Tools

1. Select any range of data.
2. An icon appears in the lower left-hand corner of the selected text as in Figure 57.

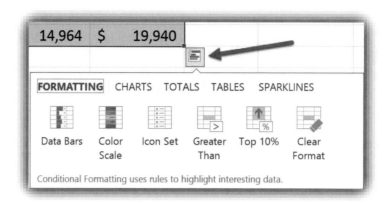

Figure 57 Quick Analysis Options

3. Select one of the tabs: **Formatting**, **Charts**, **Totals**, **Tables**, or **Sparklines**.

4. Then click on the appropriate tool to tell your story.

5. To erase any formatting that you applied (from the Formatting tab), choose **Clear Format**.

Tip #66 Print to fit one page wide

Applies to Excel 2007, Excel 2010, Excel 2013

You've been there. Ready to print your amazing spreadsheet only to see the columns break across two pages. And no matter how hard you try – and you try really, really hard –it's almost impossible to get the font small enough so that all of your columns make it onto the first page and large enough to actually read it.

Reports can carry over rows and rows of data to another page...vertically. But split the columns across multiple tables? Only in rare instances.

Put away the tape and your magnifying glass! There's a simple trick. Let's set the width for your report to one page and leave the height to Automatic.

To fit all columns on one page when printing

1. On the **Page Layout** tab, in the **Scale to fit** group, change the **Width** dropdown to 1 page as seen in Figure 58.

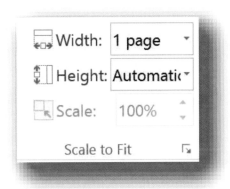

Figure 58. Page Width settings on the Page Layout tab

2. Use Print Preview to check your work.
3. If necessary, change the margins to Narrow Margins and perhaps change the settings for the page orientation and page size until you get the exact look you want.

93

Tip #67 Print column headings on every page

Applies to Excel 2007, Excel 2010, Excel 2013

Now that you've learned to how keep all of your columns on one page instead of splitting across multiple pages, it's time to focus on the rows. It's acceptable for the rows to split across multiple pages, vertically. But when it happens we need to make sure our headers are repeated on every page. Here's how.

Print column headings on every page

1. On the **Page Layout** tab, in the **Page Setup** group, click **Print Titles** as seen in Figure 59.

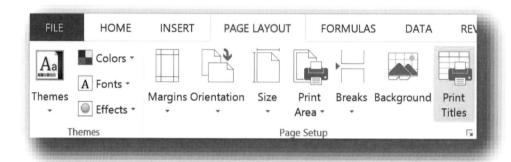

Figure 59. Print Titles command on the Page Layout ribbon

2. Click in the Rows to repeat at top field. Then, click on Row #1 in your spreadsheet (or whatever row you want to repeat at the top of each page), as seen in Figure 60, and Excel will place the appropriate reference to that row (or rows) in the Print Titles setting.

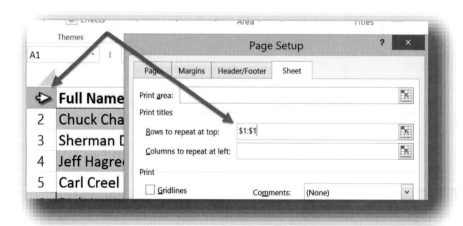

Figure 60. Print Titles setting in the Page Setup dialog box

3. Click **Ok**.

Tip #68 Send a worksheet – not the entire workbook – to a colleague

Applies to Excel 2007, Excel 2010, Excel 2013

When you need to send a colleague your spreadsheet but you don't want to send the entire workbook, copy the one worksheet they need to a new workbook and then send the new workbook (with that one worksheet) to your colleague.

To copy a worksheet to a new workbook

1. Right-click the sheet tab you wish to share and choose **Move or Copy…**
2. Click the **To book:** dropdown and select **(new book)**.
3. Very important! Check the box **Create a copy** as seen in Figure 61.

Figure 61. Move or copy worksheet dialog box: This option MUST be checked

4. Click **Ok**. The title bar at the top of your worksheet should say Book1 or similar, herein referred to as Book#.
5. Go back to your original workbook and confirm that the sheet was copied (as described in Step 3) and that the sheet is still in the original workbook.

95

To send the worksheet as an email attachment

1. Make sure you are in the new Book# workbook.
2. On the **File** tab, click **Share**.
3. Click **Email**, then click **Send as Attachment** and complete your email message.
4. Return to Book# and save, if necessary, or close without saving only after you have confirmed the sheet you just emailed is still in your original workbook.

PowerPoint 2013

Don't reinvent the wheel.

Tip #69 Start with a template

Applies to PowerPoint 2007, PowerPoint 2010, PowerPoint 2013

If you need design or content ideas for your presentation, using a template is a great way to inspire your creativity, not to mention help you save hours of time! Templates contain design themes, slide layouts, as well as boiler plate content.

Boiler plate content is the main distinction between a Theme and a Template. Themes only include the design elements such as colors, fonts, backgrounds, layouts, and slide masters. Whereas, Templates would include everything in a Theme, plus have 1 or more slides with sample content, such as welcome and conclusion slides, agenda slides, charts and diagrams, etc. Listed here are some standard templates that are included with PowerPoint.

Category	Templates
Business	Business Plan Business Strategy Business Cards
Education	Quiz Show Student Flyer
Medical	Health and Fitness Medical Brochure
Photo Albums	Graduation Family Reunion Wedding

Your company may have standard templates, such as new hire training, monthly status meetings, board of directors meeting, etc.

If you are in the marketing department and you need to create a branded slide deck for all employees, you wouldn't need a Template. You need a Theme since Themes are where you define your colors, fonts, backgrounds, layouts and slide masters. See Tip #70 on how to use and modify a Theme.

To create a presentation from a template

1. On the **File** tab, select **New** to launch **Backstage** view.as seen in Figure 62.

Figure 62. New Templates option in Backstage view

2. Select one of the template options under **Suggested searches**, such as Business.
3. Once you choose your type, such as Business, you'll see a list of categories on the right. A list of thumbnails display, along with a Category listing that you can use to narrow your selection down as seen in Figure 63.

Figure 63. New Template Business Categories

4. In our example, I chose Human Resources as the Business category and then selected the Employee Orientation template as seen in Figure 64.

Figure 64 Create a Template Preview

5. The preview gives you a summary and a rating to help you decide if the template will meet your needs.

6. Click **Create** and start editing.

 To create a presentation from a template in PowerPoint 2007, click the Office button and then click **New**, and then **Installed Templates**.   Then follow steps 3 and 4 above.

 To create a presentation from a template in PowerPoint 2010, click the **File** tab, click **New** and then click the **Sample Templates** button to see the list of available templates. Or instead of clicking Sample Templates, you can use the search bar for Office.com Templates.

Tip #70 Use a design theme

Applies to PowerPoint 2007, PowerPoint 2010, PowerPoint 2013

PowerPoint themes include slide masters, slide layouts, backgrounds, color palettes, fonts and effects. You can start with one of PowerPoint's design themes or you can build and use your own.

Each Theme has four variations, which is a new feature in PowerPoint 2013. So after you select your Theme, select your variant, color palette, font set, and effects to build out a great presentation design all your own.

If you work for a company that requires that you use the company's branded slides, the recommended approach would be for your marketing department to create the Theme and then distribute that Theme to all employees so that it shows up in the list of Themes in PowerPoint.

To use a design theme

1. On the **Design** tab, in the **Themes** group, mouse over the various themes available.
2. When you find one you like, click the theme to apply to all slides.

Use a variation of the Theme

3. Next, try out one of the four variations that come with each theme: On the **Design** tab, in the **Variants** group, hover over one of the variants to get an idea of what is available.
4. Then click the variant you want to apply.

Select your colors

5. If you're happy with the colors in the Theme variation, then skip this step, otherwise on the **Design** tab, in the **Variants** group, click the drop down for the Variants and select Colors.
6. Mouse over the color sets to preview the colors.
7. Click one of the color sets to apply.

Select your fonts

8. Now it's time to select the one or two fonts you will use throughout your presentation. On the **Design** tab, in the **Variants** group, click the drop down for the Variants and select Fonts.
9. Mouse over the font sets to preview the fonts.
10. Click one of the font sets to apply.

 Note: Changing from one design theme to another means that you're also changing slide layouts. As a result, existing content on your slides may need to be adjusted. Check out the magical Reset button in Tip #75! When you apply a new Theme to your existing presentation, be sure to go through each slide and use the Reset button to adjust content if necessary.

Tip #71 Reuse or merge slides from other presentations

Applies to PowerPoint 2007, PowerPoint 2010, PowerPoint 2013

If you have ever wanted to add a slide or slides from another presentation into your current presentation, you're going to need this tip.

To reuse slides from other presentations

1. From Normal view or in Slide Sorter view, select the slide that you want the new slide to follow.
2. As if you are inserting a new slide, on the **Home** tab, in the **Slides** group, click the **New Slide** dropdown arrow.
3. Select **Reuse Slides** to open the **Reuse Slides** pane.
4. Click the **Browse** button and select **Browse File**.

5. Locate the presentation that contains the slides you want to reuse and click **Open**. This fills the **Reuse Slides** pane with the slides from that presentation.

Before inserting slides into your current presentation, decide whether you want the added slides to keep their original design format (background, font style etc.) or to follow the format of the existing presentation you are editing.

6. If you want the added slide(s) to keep its/their original formatting, click the **Keep Source Formatting** option at the very bottom of the **Reuse Slides** pane, otherwise accept the default setting, which is unchecked.
7. Then click the slide or slides you want to add to your presentation.

This tip is a great complement to Tip #72 where you can select one or more sections of slides from another presentation and insert into your new presentation.

Keep in mind that when you paste slides into your presentation, the slides will take on the same format as the destination presentation. If you want to keep the formatting of the original slides, then you want to paste with "Source Formatting". From the Paste dropdown arrow on the toolbar, click **Source Formatting**. This will not only bring in the formatting for the source slide, but its slide master and layouts!

Manage your presentation.

Tip #72 Create sections in PowerPoint

Applies to PowerPoint 2010, PowerPoint 2013

Sections allow you to group slides together so that you can nicely organize your topic or speaker slides, effortlessly navigate your presentation and easily print logical sections of slides. It was one of MY favorite features introduced in PowerPoint 2010.

Here is an example of a 27-slide presentation with sections defined for each speaker.

> ▷ Introduction (3 slides)
>
> ▷ Mr. London (7 slides)
>
> ▷ Mr. Sydney (5 slides)
>
> ▷ Ms. Austin (6 slides)
>
> ▷ Partner Spotlight (4 slides)
>
> ▷ Q&A + Wrap Up (2 slides)

You can also create sections centered on topics or the schedule for the day (ie Session 1, Break, Session 2...). Section your slides in a way that will help you organize the slides behind the scenes as well as navigate while presenting.

To create sections in your presentation

1. In either Normal or Slide Sorter view, click on the first slide you want in the new section.
2. On the **Home** tab, in the **Slides** group, click **Section**.
3. Select **Add Section** to create a new section after the current slide. Alternatively, you can right-click in front of a slide and choose **Add Section**.
4. Right-click the new section header in front of your slide and select **Rename** to give it a meaningful name.
5. Repeat the steps above to create more sections throughout your presentation.

Tip: Right-click any section name to see all the commands you have available for sections as seen in Figure 65. You can rename sections, expand and collapse sections, move sections of slides around, as well as delete a section or delete a section and its slides.

Figure 65. Section commands available when you right-click a section

To print one section of slides

1. Go to the **File** tab, click **Print** and click the **Print all slides** drop down to reveal the list of options. You will see a heading called Sections and all of your sections will be listed there as seen in Figure 66.
2. Click the Section you want to print and then configure the rest of the print out such as full slides or handouts, etc.

 Tip: I like to include a Section Header Layout slide at the beginning of each section to help the audience transition to the new agenda item, topic or next speaker. Click right after the Section, then on the **Home** tab in the **Slides** group, click **New Slide** and choose Section Header. Repeat this for all of your sections to ensure a consistent transition slide.

Figure 66. Print Dialog Box to print sections

Tip #73 Globally change your fonts or color palette for the entire presentation

Applies to PowerPoint 2007, PowerPoint 2010, PowerPoint 2013

Once way to ensure a late night at the office fixing slides is to modify fonts at the slide level. Traditionally, if you need a different font on a slide you would modify it right there on the slide. One slide at a time. That is a HUGE time waster. Instead, you'll want to modify the font at the Slide Master level. Because whatever is on the Slide Master flows down to all slide layouts and whatever is defined on a slide layout flows to the slides.

For more information about Slide Masters, see **Error! Reference source ot found.**.

To globally change the fonts in your presentation

1. On the **Design** tab, in the **Variants** group, click the dropdown arrow and select **Fonts**.
2. Select the font set you want, which will update the Slide Master and its layouts with the correct heading and body fonts. If you don't see your favorite Font Set, then click **Customize Fonts** at the bottom of the list to create your own set. Be sure to rename and save your Font Set, which will now be available in Excel and Word.

You can alternatively change fonts globally in Slide Master View. On the **View** tab, in the **Master Views** group, click **Slide Master** to change to Slide Master View. The tab to the right of the **File** tab will say **Slide Master** as seen in Figure 67.

On the **Slide Master** tab, in the **Background** group, click the **Fonts** drop down to view the various Font Sets that come with PowerPoint.

Follow step 2 above if you want to create a custom font set.

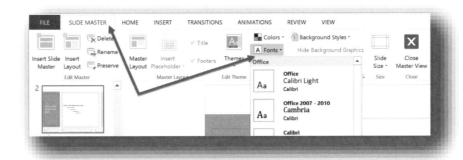

Figure 67. Slide Master View > Change Fonts

In Excel 2010 or earlier, on the **Design** tab, in the **Themes** group, click the **Fonts** drop down option to view all the Font Sets.

Tip #74 Create one slide show for multiple audiences

Applies to PowerPoint 2007, PowerPoint 2010, PowerPoint 2013

Rather than creating multiple files of your presentation for different audiences or hiding slides within your presentation, you can create one PowerPoint file that includes multiple slide shows for various audiences.

For example, an executive audience might only need to see the high-level overview slides and then another audience needs to see both the high-level overview and the more detailed slides. You can do this without hiding slides and without having to create and manage two separate slide decks.

To create a custom slide show for each audience

1. On the **Slide Show** tab, in the **Start Slide Show** group, click **Custom Slide Show**.
2. Click **New...**

3. In the Define New Slide Show window, as seen in Figure 68, type a name that best describes the custom slide show in the **Slide Show Name** box.
4. From the **Slides in presentation** list, select the slide you want to include in the custom slide show and click the **Add** button. Repeat for all the slides you need for this custom slide show.
5. Use the move up and move down buttons to reorder the slides in the list.
6. When done, click **Ok** and **Close**.
7. Repeat for each custom presentation.

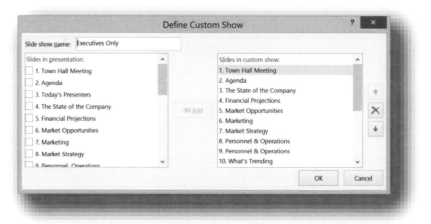

Figure 68. Define Custom Slide Show dialog box

To launch a custom slide show

1. On the **Slide Show** tab, in the **Start Slide Show** group, click **Custom Slide Show**.
2. Select the custom show you wish to run.
3. Click **Show**.

   Or

1. Use the [F5] keyboard shortcut to run your main slide show.
2. Right-click the current slide and mouse over **Custom Show**.
3. Select the custom show you wish to run.

Tip #75 Fix a problem slide using the magical Reset button

Applies to PowerPoint 2007, PowerPoint 2010, PowerPoint 2013

The Reset button has to be the best kept secret in all of PowerPoint history. In my nearly 20 years of supporting PowerPoint users, 80-90% of the time knowledge of the reset button would have saved hours of time, reduced stress and prevented missed deadlines.

For instance, suppose you accidentally nudged the slide title out of position. Or someone changed the font on the slide to something other than what the font SHOULD be. Or you have a vast buffet of inconsistencies (colors, fonts, bullets). Rather than individually fix each item, click the Reset button to reset the slide to the defined Slide Layout. It's brilliant!

No, it's magical.

To fix a problem slide using the magical Rest button

1. On the **Home** tab, in the **Slide** group, click **Reset** as seen in Figure 69 to reset the current slide to the definition of the layout.

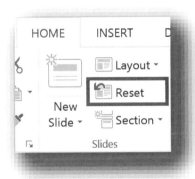

Figure 69. The PowerPoint Reset Button

2. If it doesn't reset to the right layout, you may need to change the layout of the slide by going to the **Home** tab, in the **Slide** group, click **Layout** and apply the correct layout.

3. Once you've reset the slide to match the layout, you may need to make a few adjustments but thankfully, the fonts, bullets, colors and positioning of content should now be consistent with the other slides, or at least consistent with the Design Theme.

4. If the content doesn't go with the layout you've selected, then you may need to modify the layout itself, which is defined in the next Tip, or create a new layout as described in 0.

Tip #76 Format multiple slides at once by modifying the layout

Applies to PowerPoint 2007, PowerPoint 2010, PowerPoint 2013

Let me ask you this. If you must change the 1st level bullet style of all the slides in your presentation, would you rather (a) take the time and effort to change the bullets on each slide individually or (b) make the change on one slide, which cascades down to all of the other slides that have bullets?

The obvious answer is (b) on one slide. But most people don't approach it this way because they are unaware of this next tip: how to modify the slide master.

In this example, we'll change the bullet style for the first level bullet in our bulleted lists. If you want to change your fonts, see 0.

Make a global change to your slides by modifying the slide master

1. On the **View** tab, in the **Master Views** group, click **Slide Master**. Now that you are in Slide Master view, notice all of the layouts on the left hand side of your screen. The screenshot below shows the Slide Master (with the red star) and all of its corresponding layouts. Not all of the corresponding layouts have bullets. Those that do, are identified in the screenshot by a blue star.

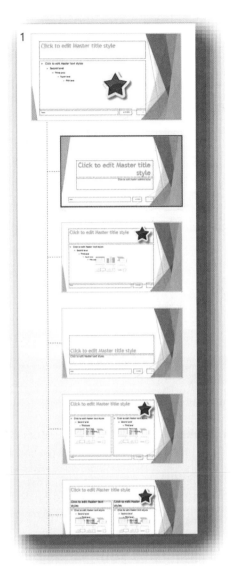

1. In order to modify the first level bullet for all of the bulleted slides at once, you can simply make the change on the Slide Master (my slide with the red star), which will cascade down to any layout (my slides with the blue star) that has bullets. Any slides in your presentation using a bulleted list layout, will then have the new bullet!

2. Make sure you have selected the Slide Master slide (the top level slide above all of the layouts).

3. Click in the first bulleted line and on the **Home** tab, in the **Paragraph** group, click the drop down for the bullets. Choose a different bullet as seen in Figure 70.

Figure 70. Changing bullets on our Slide Master

All of the layouts with a bulleted list will now include this new bullet and as a result, all of the slides based on those layouts will now include the new bullet.

4. Close out of Slide Master view. On the **Slide Master** tab, in the **Close** group, click **Close Master View**.

5. If one of your slides does not get updated with the new bullet, use the magical Reset button to reset it to the layout. See Tip #75, if you need more help using the reset button.

Tip #77 Create a new slide layout

Applies to PowerPoint 2007, PowerPoint 2010, PowerPoint 2013

Slide layouts are a great tool to help you organize content on your slides consistently throughout your presentation but what do you do when there isn't a slide layout to meet your needs? For example, during your monthly business reviews, managers must include a standard slide with a table, a chart and bulleted text to describe their business? Rather than insert each one of those items manually to slides and spend time aligning the objects on the slide, you can create a new slide layout to do most – well, ALL – of the work for you.

To create a new slide layout

1. On the **View** tab, in the **Master Views** group, click **Slide Master**.
2. On the **Slide Master** tab, in the **Edit Master** group, click **Insert Layout** to insert a new slide.
3. To add placeholders, on the **Slide Master** tab, in the **Master Layout** group, click the dropdown arrow to the right of **Insert Placeholder**. As you mouse over a placeholder, it gives you a definition.
4. Select a placeholder, which turns your mouse into a crosshair, and then draw the new placeholder on your slide in the preferred location.
5. Repeat steps 3 and 4 for all the placeholders you wish to add to the new slide layout.
6. Rearrange and resize, if necessary.
7. To rename your new layout slide:
8. Right-click the slide in the left pane of Slide Master view and select **Rename Layout**.
9. Give your layout a descriptive name and click **Rename**.
10. On the **Slide Master** tab, in the **Close** group, click **Close Master View**.

To insert a new slide using the new slide layout

1. On the **Home** tab, in the **Slides** group, click the **New Slide** dropdown arrow.
2. Select your new slide layout.

To apply the new slide layout to an existing slide

1. Navigate to the slide you wish to apply the new slide layout to.
2. On the **Home** tab, in the **Slides** group, click the **Layout** dropdown arrow.
3. Select your new slide layout.

Tip #78 Convert text to SmartArt

Applies to PowerPoint 2007, PowerPoint 2010, PowerPoint 2013

Tired of bulleted lists? Chances are, so is your audience! Make your ideas stand out by using SmartArt, which was first introduced in Office 2007.

SmartArt uses your existing bulleted list and magically converts them to a diagram or illustration that is much easier to organize and present.

And they are easy and fun!

To convert your text to SmartArt

1. Select the text you want to convert to SmartArt
2. Right-click the selection and select **Convert to SmartArt** to view a gallery of SmartArt graphics.

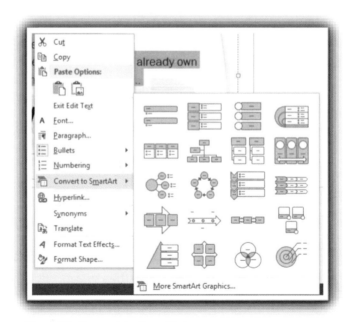

Figure 71. Convert to SmartArt

3. Select the graphic you want or click **More SmartArt Graphics…** to view the entire library of SmartArt by category as seen in Figure 72.

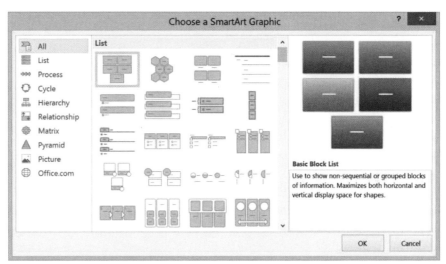

Figure 72. SmartArt Gallery

4. A separate dialog box pops up to allow you to easily add or rearrange the points on your slide.
5. Click the "X" in the top right-hand corner when you are finished editing the points.
6. To readjust the SmartArt points, open the Text pane by clicking the text handle on the left side of the SmartArt as seen in Figure 73.

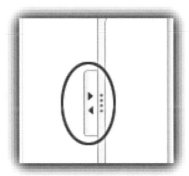

Figure 73. SmartArt Text handle

This tip meets the "Including Illustrations and Graphics in a Document" objective of the Microsoft® Office Specialist exams.

Tip #79 Add compelling transitions to your slides

Applies to PowerPoint 2007, PowerPoint 2010, PowerPoint 2013

Adding transitions in your presentation visually guides your audience through the major sections or topics of the presentation to help increase the effectiveness of your message.

Suppose that all of your slides transition the same way with a simple wipe transition. You can add a different, more compelling transition for each of your main topics to visually cue your audience that you're moving to the next major point in your presentation or presenter.

To add transitions to your key point slides

1. Switch to Slide Sorter view. On the **View** tab, in the **Presentation Views** group, click **Slide Sorter**.
2. Click your first key point slide. Hold down [CTRL] and click each of the other main topic slides.
3. Once all your main topic slides have been selected, add the transition. On the **Transitions** tab, in the in the **Transition to This Slide** group select one of the transitions. You will have to either scroll through the list or click the **More** button below the Transition scroll bars as seen in Figure 74.
4. (Optional) To apply a simple transition for all your slides, select all by using [CTRL]+[A] and then click the **Transition** tab, and in the **Transition to This Slide** group select one of the transitions.

Figure 74. The More button in the Transition to This Slide group.

In PowerPoint 2010 and PowerPoint 2013, you can also select transitions from the Exciting or Dynamic Content category for your key point slides.

 **Transitions** is located on the **Animations** tab in PowerPoint 2007, in the **Transition to this slide** group.

Become an instant graphic artist.

Warning... this section may be harmful to your time management. Many users love how easy it is to work with images in PowerPoint and use the time they saved from the previous tips in this book on these fun tools.

Tip #80 Remove the background in an image

Applies to PowerPoint 2010, PowerPoint 2013

When adding images to a slide, or within an Excel or Word document, there will be times when you need to remove the background so that it is transparent. The Remove Background feature was introduced in Office 2010, and eliminated the need for a third party tool such as a graphic design program to fix your picture.

Remove the background in an image

1. Select the image in your presentation (or Excel or Word file).
2. On the **Format** tab, in the **Adjust** group, click **Remove Background**.

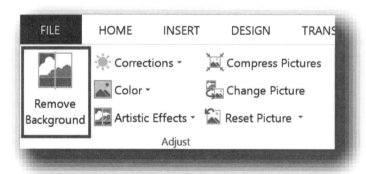

Figure 75. Remove Background button

3. Once you choose **Remove Background**, your image will be outlined. Anything in magenta will be marked for removal. Use the handles on the outlined border to reposition the area of the image you want to keep.
4. If an area you don't want to keep is NOT magenta, click the **Mark Areas to Remove** button on the **Background Removal** tab as seen in Figure 76. Your cursor will change into a pencil. Use the pencil tool to

draw a straight line through the area you want to remove. Repeat for all areas you want to remove.

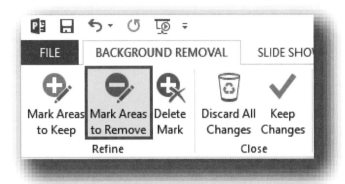

Figure 76. Remove Background Commands

5. If an area you WANT to keep is magenta, click the **Mark Areas to Keep** button on the **Background Removal** tab. Your cursor will change into a pencil. Use the pencil tool to draw a straight line through the area you want to keep. Repeat for all areas you want to keep.
6. When you are done, click the **Keep Changes** button on the **Background Removal** tab.

Tip #81 Style your pictures effortlessly

Applies to PowerPoint 2007, PowerPoint 2010, PowerPoint 2013

First introduced in Office 2007, picture styles give your images a professional look with the press of a button.

To style your pictures instantly

1. Select an image in your presentation. Notice the **Picture Tools** contextual tabs on the ribbon.
2. On the **Format** tab, in the **Picture Styles** group, mouse over one of the picture styles to see a preview of the style. Scroll through the list or click the **More** button below the Picture Styles scroll bars as seen in Figure 77.

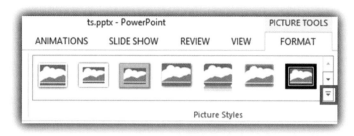

Figure 77. The More button in the Picture Styles group

 Meets the "Including Illustrations and Graphics in a Document" objective of the Microsoft® Office Specialist exam.

Tip #82 Add artistic effects to your text

Applies to PowerPoint 2007, PowerPoint 2010, PowerPoint 2013

To make certain statements stand out on the slide such as a call to action "Silence your Cell Phones" or "Join Today," you can easily add artistic effects.

To add artistic effects to your text

1. Select the text you want to affect. Notice the **Drawing Tools** contextual tabs on the ribbon.
2. On the **Format** tab, in the **Word Art Styles** group, select one of the Word Art styles in the gallery or select the **Text Effects** button.

 This tip meets the "Including Illustrations and Graphics in a Document" objective of the Microsoft® Office Specialist exams.

Tip #83 Draw straight lines, perfect squares and perfect circles

Applies to PowerPoint 2007, PowerPoint 2010, PowerPoint 2013

I can't draw a straight line or perfect square and circle to save my life. Luckily my life doesn't depend on it. But if it did, I'd be safe because of a simple [Shift] key.

To draw straight lines

1. On the **Insert** tab, in the **Illustrations** group, select **Shapes** and click the line you wish to draw.
2. Hold down [SHIFT] as you draw the line and you'll never have a crooked line.

To draw perfect squares and circles

1. On the **Insert** tab, in the **Illustrations** group, select **Shapes** and click the rectangle or oval shape.
2. Hold down the [SHIFT] key as you draw the rectangle or oval and the shape snaps into a perfect square or circle.

Tip #84 Connect shapes using lines and arrows

Applies to PowerPoint 2007, PowerPoint 2010, PowerPoint 2013

When you need to draw a connecting line between two shapes, you want to be sure that the line is attached to the shapes so that when you move either shape, the line moves with them.

To dynamically connect two shapes together using a line or arrow

1. Select the first shape and then hold [SHIFT] down and select the second shape.
2. On the **Insert** tab, in the **Illustrations** group, select **Shapes** and click the line you wish to draw.
3. Mouse over the first shape's handle to find the dots at each "target" handle for the shape and then choose one to start the line. Click,

holding the mouse down and drag from that target handle to the other shape's target handle.

4. When you let the mouse go, the two shapes are connected with the line and two green dots show the connection points of the two shapes as seen in Figure 78.

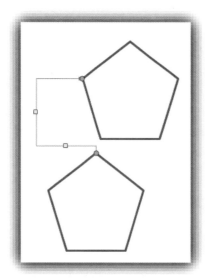

Figure 78 Dynamic Connection of Two Shapes

In PowerPoint 2007 and PowerPoint 2010 the connector dots are red instead of green.

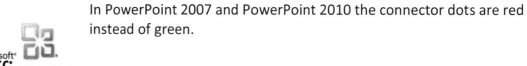

Present like the pros.

Tip #85 Use keyboard shortcuts to run your slide show

From the beginning

Applies to PowerPoint 2007, PowerPoint 2010, PowerPoint 2013

No matter what slide you're on in your presentation, you're one keystroke away from launching your presentation from the very beginning.

To run your slide show from the beginning using a keyboard shortcut

- Press the [F5] key from anywhere in your presentation.

From the current slide

Applies to PowerPoint 2007, PowerPoint 2010, PowerPoint 2013

If you want to run through your presentation starting with your current slide, add the shift key to the keyboard shortcut mentioned in the last tip.

To run your slide show from the current slide using a keyboard shortcut

- Navigate to the slide you wish to start from and press [SHIFT]+[F5].

Tip #86 Use presenter view

Applies to PowerPoint 2013

Presenter View gives you – the presenter – a view of your notes and upcoming slides when you are presenting, while your audience sees only your slides. Presenter View has been around a while, but there are some major improvements in PowerPoint 2013. Not only does the interface look dramatically different, you no longer have to connect to a projector or second monitor to work in Presenter View. You can practice on your laptop or computer using Presenter View before the big presentation day arrives.

Switch to Presenter View in PowerPoint 2013

- When you connect a projector or another monitor, there is no set up required. Simply run the Slide Show using F5 or Shift+F5 as described in Tip #85.
- If you are NOT connected to a projector or another monitor, run the Slide Show on your screen and click the Control Bar (three dots) on the bottom left hand corner of your current slide and choose **Show Presenter View** as seen in Figure 79.

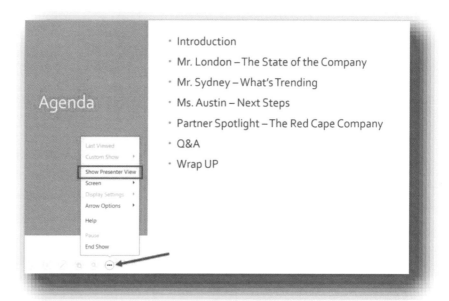

Figure 79. Show Presenter View during a slide show

Switch between Presenter View and Duplicate

- When you need to revert to duplicate screens again, use the **Display Settings** option at the top of the Presenter View and choose **Duplicate Slide Shows**. This only works when you connect to a projector or 2nd monitor.

- If you have only one monitor, click the **Presenter View Options** button and choose **Hide Presenter View**.

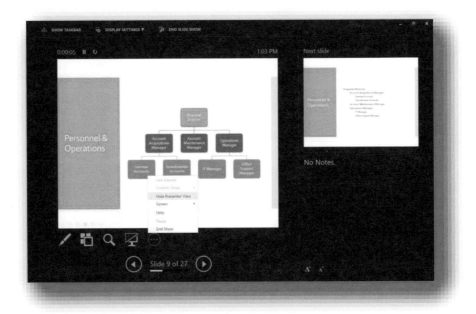

Figure 80. Presenter View options within Presenter View

Use Presenter View tools – available at the bottom of the screen

- Move through slides – Use the arrows
- View all slides (and sections) in your presentation – Click **See all Slides** button.
- Zoom into a slide – Use the magnifying glass.
- Point or write on slides – Use the pencil icon.
- Hide or unhide current slide – Click the **Black or unblack slide show** button.

Figure 81. Presenter View - Move through slides

Figure 82. Presenter View - Point or write on slides

Figure 83. Presenter View - See all slides (and Sections!)

Figure 84. Presenter View - Zoom ino the slide

Figure 85. Presenter View - Black or unblack slide show

Figure 86. Presenter View - More slide show options

In PowerPoint 2007 and PowerPoint 2010 you must be connected to a second display such as a projector or a second monitor to use Presenter View. Once you have a second display connected, on the **Slide Show** tab, in the **Monitors** group, check **Use Presenter View**, then run your slide show: **Slide Show** tab > **Start Slide Show** group > **From Beginning**. The interface is different than PowerPoint 2013, the many of the commands are available as seen in Figure 87.

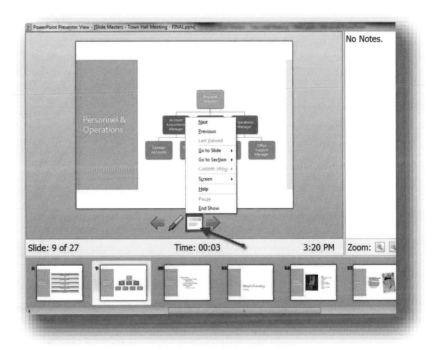

Figure 87. PowerPoint 2007/2010 Presenter View

Tip #87 Jump to a slide (or section) while presenting

Applies to PowerPoint 2007, PowerPoint 2010, PowerPoint 2013

You've been there. In the middle of presenting a concept or answering an audience member's question, you realize that you need to show a specific slide to illustrate a point that you're trying to make. Or perhaps you need to resume your meeting at a specific location in your deck. Here's the best way for you to get to the slide or section that you need right away, without stumbling.

Jump to a slide or section during a presentation

1. If you haven't done so already, run the slide show by using [F5].
2. Right-click your current slide and select **See All Slides**.
3. Click the Section on the left to view all the slides in that section.
4. Then click the slide you need and you're ready to go!

In PowerPoint 2007 and PowerPoint 2010, right click a slide while you are presenting in Slide Show view and choose either **Go to Slide** or **Go to Section**, and then the appropriate slide or section.

Tip #88 Zoom in on a slide

Applies to PowerPoint 2013

Does your slide have detailed information that might be difficult for the folks in the back of the room to see? You're in luck! The new Zoom feature in PowerPoint 2013, is the perfect tool for you to zoom in on important information that you won't want anyone to miss.

Zoom in on a slide while presenting

1. While presenting in slide show view, move your mouse to the bottom left hand side of the slide to see the Presenter tools available, as seen in Figure 88.

2. Click the magnifying glass tool to get into Zoom mode and then click the area of the slide you want to zoom in on.
3. You can use the hand cursor to move around.
4. Once done, click the slide once to get out of Zoom mode.

Figure 88. Slide show Zoom command

Tip #89 Start an online meeting from PowerPoint

Applies to PowerPoint 2010, PowerPoint 2013

When you need to deliver an internal presentation to a team or even to just one person, you can use Microsoft Lync to quickly project your slides to others. This tip assumes that you have Microsoft Lync for international communication and collaboration.

Start an online meeting from PowerPoint

1. While in your presentation, go to the **File** tab, click **Share**, **Present Online**, and Present Online as seen in Figure 89.

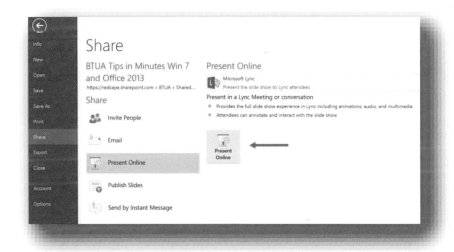

Figure 89. Backstage view for PowerPoint - Share and Present Online

2. Click **Start a New Meeting** or choose an existing one.
3. Choose your preferred audio, if necessary.

4. Invite people to the meeting and start presenting. The attendee(s) can see your PowerPoint desk as you advance through the slides.

5. In Lync 2013, click **Stop Presenting** when you are finished or simply end the Lync meeting.

Outlook 2013

Reduce your email volume.

Tip #90 Instantly remove redundant messages using Clean Up

Applies to Outlook 2010, Outlook 2013

Chances are, your mailbox has more messages in it than you'd like and it can be quite overwhelming to see how many messages are sitting there awaiting your response or waiting to be moved or deleted. The good news is many of those messages are redundant and can be quickly deleted with one press of a button.

What are redundant messages? Imagine you and I are sending messages back and forth about a project that we're working on together. For this one conversation, you have four messages from me in your inbox and I have three messages from you In my inbox. It's your turn to respond to me. Looking at your inbox, because the last message I sent you contains the entire conversation, the other three messages from me are considered redundant. There isn't anything in those first three messages that isn't in the last message. So you can clean up our conversation by deleting the first three messages. But we're not going to do it manually. Because we want to do this to all conversations in our Inbox or in all of our folders and subfolders.

Before I walk you through the clean up process, I need to point out two things.

Attachments: If a message in a conversation has an attachment, it isn't considered redundant and therefore, it won't be deleted. For instance, if the first message I sent you included an attachment, the clean up process would keep the email with the attachment (the first email), plus the last email. It would delete the second and third emails.

Split Conversations: Additionally, if our conversation had multiple people on the thread and two people separately responded to the same email, thereby creating a split conversation, those emails would not be considered redundant and would remain in your inbox or folder.

 Optional Setting: Before you begin deleting redundant messages, I recommend that you create a Clean Up folder that you can refer to if you want to analyze what is being deleted. Otherwise, the messages will, by default, get moved to your Deleted Items folder. I will show you how to do this in Step 5 below.

Use Clean Up to quickly reduce your email volume

1. View your Inbox. If you want to just clean up one conversation, be sure to click on a message in that conversation first. Otherwise, just click on any message in your inbox.
   a. TIP: Make a note about how many messages you currently have in your inbox so you can compare to the number of messages remaining in your Inbox after the Clean Up process.
2. On the **Home** tab, in the **Delete** group, click **Clean Up** as seen in Figure 90.

Figure 90. Clean Up button

3. You have three options:
   a. **Clean up conversation** – Only removes redundant messages in the conversation you have selected.

b. **Clean up folder** – Removes redundant messages for the folder you are currently in, such as your inbox.

c. **Clean up folders and subfolders** – Removes all redundant messages throughout your mailbox.

4. For your first time, let's remove redundant messages from your Inbox. Choose **Clean Up Folder** to remove all redundant messages in your inbox. You will receive a pop up message to confirm clean up as seen in Figure 91.

Figure 91. Clean Up folder confirmation

5. Before you click **Clean Up Folder**, let's change where the redundant messages are going to be moved to. By default, all redundant messages will be moved to Deleted Items. We want to create a Clean Up folder of our own. So click **Settings** as seen in Figure 91, which opens the Outlook Options dialog box as seen in Figure 92.

Figure 92. Clean Up folder - Outlook Options dialog box

6. Click the **Browse...** button and create a new folder as a subfolder of your Deleted Items folder as seen in Figure 93. Then click **Ok** to confirm all dialog boxes.

Figure 93. Clean Up Folder Settings - Select Folder

If your Deleted Items folder gets emptied every time you close Outlook, the new Clean Up folder may get deleted as well, if you create it as a subfolder of your Deleted Items. In this case, you should consider creating a Clean Up folder as a subfolder of your Inbox instead.

7. Once you're done creating the Clean up folder and saving it as the default folder, you should now be back at the Clean Up Folder confirmation as seen in Figure 91. Click **Clean up Folder** to complete the action.

8. Next, take a look at the number of messages in your inbox and compare it to what you started with. You can also navigate to your Clean Up folder that you created in step 5 above, and see how many redundant messages you had.

I recommend using the Clean Up button 2-3 times a day and choosing Folders & Subfolders so that you are constantly reducing your email volume and freeing up space.

Tip #91 Ignore conversations without hurting anyone's feelings

Applies to Outlook 2010, Outlook 2013

One of the features introduced in Outlook 2010, is the Ignore button allowing you to disregard an entire conversation without damaging any relationships. When you Ignore a conversation in Outlook, related messages in the conversation are moved to the Deleted items. Additionally, any incoming messages for that conversation will automatically move to the Deleted items. This is one of the best and easiest ways to triage your mail in the mornings and throughout the day.

If you mistakenly ignored the wrong conversation thread, you can always remove the ignore command from the conversation and messages will appear back in your inbox.

To ignore an email conversation

1. Select one of the messages in the conversation.
2. On the **Home** tab, in the **Delete** group click **Ignore**. All of the messages in that conversation will be moved to your Deleted Items.

Figure 94. The Ignore button on the Home ribbon

To stop ignoring an email conversation

1. Go to your Deleted Items folder.
2. Select one of the messages in the thread that you ignored by mistake and click **Ignore** again to turn it off. New messages will no longer be deleted automatically.

Save time for yourself and others.

Tip #92 Reply with a meeting

Applies to Outlook 2010, Outlook 2013

If you receive an email message from your manager or a customer asking to set up a meeting, you are one click away from getting it on everyone's calendar. You get the meeting set up in a jiffy and they will love how efficient you are!

Another benefit of the Reply with Meeting command is that it collectively reduces email volume for both you and the recipient(s) because you no longer have to go back and forth to set and confirm meetings.

Additional benefits include:

- Details from the email message will automatically be copied to your meeting request
- Anyone on the email thread will automatically be added as an attendee (you can always remove them during the meeting set up)

To reply with a meeting

1. On the **Home** tab, in the **Respond** group, click **Meeting**. Outlook will generate a meeting item and populate the following fields:
   a. Meeting Subject = Email Subject
   b. Meeting details = Email body
   c. Meeting attendees = Email recipients and sender

Figure 95. Reply with Meeting button

2. Add the date, time and location information.

Don't forget to set the correct date and time for the meeting! This is a common mistake.

3. Click. **Send**.

Tip #93 Reduce time zone errors

Applies to Outlook 2007, Outlook 2010, Outlook 2013

In today's workplace, it's inevitable that you will set up meetings or conference calls for yourself or for attendees in various time zones and you certainly don't want to make a mistake. Additionally, if you travel between time zones, you'll want to ensure that your flight gets added to your calendar correctly, so that no matter where you are in the world, your calendar (and your Smartphone) will always be correct.

Rather than convert the time zone in your head, which is risky behavior in my opinion, let Outlook do the work for you.

In this example, we'll walk through how to correctly add a flight that covers multiple time zones to your calendar. Your flight leaves Dallas at 8:45AM Dallas local time and arrives in San Francisco at 10:30AM San Francisco local time. Your goal is to set the start time in Outlook as Central Time and the end time as Pacific Time so that everything syncs beautifully.

Reduce time zone errors

1. Create a new appointment on your calendar or modify an existing one.
2. Enter the details for the subject, location and date.
3. Display the Time Zone fields: On the **Appointment** tab, in the **Options** group, click **Time Zones** as seen in Figure 96.

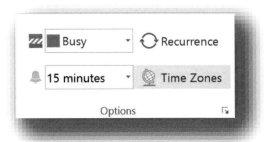

Figure 96. Time Zones command in Outlook

4. For the Start Time, enter **8:45 AM** and set the time zone to **Central Time (US & Canada)**.

5. For the End Time, enter **11:30 AM** and set the time zone to **Pacific Time (US & Canada)**.

6. Make any necessary changes to the appointment and click **Save & Close**.

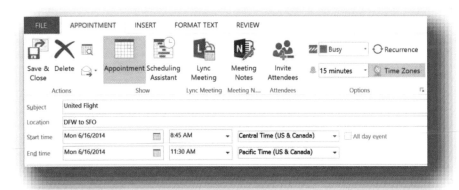

Figure 97. Time zones set for DFW to SFO flight

When you land in a different time zone other than your local time zone, your mobile device will automatically adjust to the new time zone but your laptop will not. This means that when you open Outlook on your computer, you're viewing your calendar in your original time zone.

In order to change your laptop to the new local time zone, click on the date/time in the bottom right hand corner of your computer screen. Click **Change date and time settings....** In your **Windows Date and Time** dialog box as seen in Figure 98, on the **Date and Time** tab, click **Change Time Zone** and choose the new local time zone that you're in and click **Ok**.

Figure 98. Windows Date and Time dialog box

Tip #94 Create clickable links for mobile users

Applies to Outlook 2007, Outlook 2010, Outlook 2013

When you view email or details of an appointment on your smartphone, you've probably noticed by now that phone numbers and addresses are displayed as hyperlinks (as seen in Figure 99). A hyperlinked address provides one-click access to navigation and a hyperlinked phone provides one-click calling. It's not only convenient, it's safer for those who are driving and trying to find their way to that important meeting.

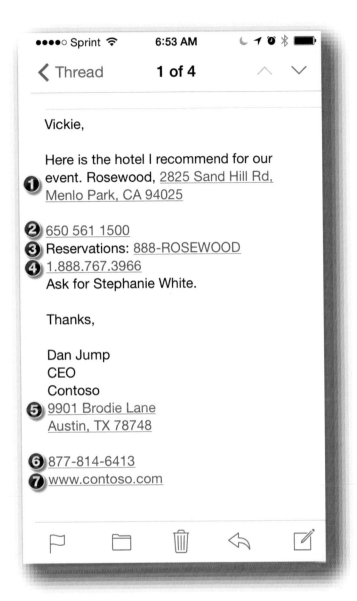

Figure 99. Active hyperlinks for phone and addresses on a mobile device

Let's take a closer look at what mobile users see when you either send them an email or store the details in a meeting request by examining Figure 99.

1. **Address on one line** – When you type an address on one single line, versus a block, you still get the active hyperlink on the smartphone. Be careful though. If you include a building number or suite number the hyperlink will break and it won't be correct. Instead, put the building or suite number either before or after the address.

2. **Phone number with spaces** – Should work just fine on most mobile devices. But test it out! Send yourself an email with the phone number in the format of your choice and view and/or test the hyperlink on your phone to see if it works properly.

3. **Alphanumeric phone numbers** – Yay! Our smartphone recognized an alphanumeric phone number. But beware, not all of the smartphones out there do so be sure to include the alternate numeric version along with the alphanumeric one just to be safe.

4. **Phone numbers formatted with periods** – Our smartphone also recognized a phone number even with periods instead of dashes. Historically, not all smartphones did but it looks like it many new mobile systems are now creating active hyperlinks for phone numbers formatted with periods successfully. My recommendation though is to use the proper format such as dashes and spaces, versus the periods just to be safe.

5. **Address block** - When you type an address in standard block format, the hyperlink works great! Be careful though. If you include a building number or suite number anywhere in the address block the hyperlink will break and it won't be correct. Your meeting attendees may get lost because the navigation won't work for broken links! Instead, put the building or suite number either before or after the address.

6. **Phone numbers formatted with dashes** – work just fine as well. All smartphones recognize dashes and will create the hyperlink correctly.

7. **Website** – as expected, this works just great on smartphones!

Tip #95 Create 1-click links into a conference call

A member of one of my audiences shared this next tip with me and I've been spreading the word about it ever since. I just wish I knew her name so I can give her credit for this next awesome tip!

When you or your manager needs to connect to a conference bridge while you are away from your desk – perhaps you're driving or in another building, etc... – you can obviously use your smartphone to dial the number for you but it won't autodial the participant or host passcode for you. This means that you will have to write the passcode down before you make the call so that you can dial it in when prompted.

An easier and more convenient way – not to mention, cooler – is to create a hyperlink that will not only dial the conference call number but the participant or host passcode for you, too! Cool, right? Who doesn't want 1-click entry into a conference call?

In our example, the conference call number is 877-814-6413. The participant passcode is 98765, and then #. The 1-click format will look like this:

1-877-814-6413,,,98765#

The three commas represent a pause of three seconds. You can use two commas for a two second pause.

Note: Consider your audience. If they are not familiar with this format, you'll want to store the customary format in the Location field of your meeting (or wherever you typically store it) and then add a line in your meeting notes similar to this so that there is no confusion.

1-Click Call-In for Mobile Devices: 1-877-814-6413,,,98765#

Create 1-click links into a conference call

1. Create a new meeting or modify and existing one.
2. In the location field, type your standard conference call info.
3. In the Meeting Notes field, type the following phrase: **<u>1-Click Call-In for Mobile Devices:</u>**
4. And then type the conference call number, three commas and the participant passcode. No need to include spaces.
5. Optional. If employees traditionally need to use the pound key when dialing in, then add the pound or hash tag to the end of the passcode. So it should look like this: 1-Click Call-In for Mobile Devices: 1-877-814-6413,,,98765#

Tip #96 Set your mail to expire

Applies to Outlook 2007, Outlook 2010, Outlook 2013

Be kind to your colleagues and set expiration dates for timely emails. Messages that expire will display in the recipient's inbox as "crossed off" giving them a strong visual cue that the message is no longer relevant. This allows your colleagues to stay focused on what matters most.

This tip might help you get nominated for coworker or employee of the month!

Figure 100. Expired message from Karen Berg sitting in an Inbox

To set the expiration date and time for a message

1. Start drafting your email message.
2. On the **Options** tab, in the **More Options** group, click the dialog box launcher button as seen in Figure 101. This launches the **Properties** dialog box.

Figure 101. Dialog box launcher for More Options

3. Click the **Expires after** check box and type in the specific date and time that the message expires.
4. Click **Close**.
5. Click **Send** when you're done drafting your message. You won't see any difference on your end but your recipient's will! And they will be your biggest fan because of it.

Tip #97 Search for email using the powerful Search Bar

Applies to Outlook 2010, Outlook 2013

It can be a daunting task searching for the email or attachment you need. You probably ask yourself, "What folder is that email in?" or "Where did that attachment go?"

Find what you're looking for in a jiffy by using the Search bar in your Inbox. The Search feature includes Scope which helps you expand or narrow your search throughout your mailbox, and Refinements which allow you to select exactly what you're looking for.

Search for email using the Search Bar

1. While in your Inbox, click the Search field at the very top of your message list as seen in Figure 102. Alternatively, you can use the [Ctrl]+[E] keyboard shortcut.

Figure 102. Outlook Search Bar

2. Once you click in the Search field, it will activate the Search ribbon as seen in Figure 103.

Figure 103. Outlook Search Ribbon

3. To change the scope to include all mailboxes, choose **All Mailboxes**, otherwise leave it on the default setting **Current Folder**.

4. To search for a message from a person, click the **From** button, which places the proper search code in the Search field. Then type in the person's name or a partial email address.

5. To find only those messages that have attachments from that person, click **Has Attachments**.

6. Then hit [Enter].

Tip #98 Quickly find that attachment using the People Pane

Applies to Outlook 2010, Outlook 2013

Suppose you are on a conference call and your customer asks if you have the file they sent last week. Rather than frantically search or scroll through hundreds of emails to find it, use the Outlook People Pane to find any and all attachments from a sender in an instant. As long as you can find one email from the sender, you have access to all of their attachments – even files from last year!

First, let's turn on the People Pane!

Turn on the People Pane

1. Both the Reading Pane and People Pane must be turned on. From your Inbox, on the **View** tab, in the **Layout** group, click **Reading Pane**, and then click **Right**.

2. On the **View** tab, in the **People Pane** group, click **People Pane**, and then click **Normal**. When you have a message selected in the message list (as seen in Figure 104), the body of the message will display in the

Reading Pane and the People Pane will be displayed for the sender
below the Reading Pane.

Figure 104. Outlook Reading Pane and People Pane turned on

To quickly find an attachment using the People Pane

1. To find the attachment your customer or colleague sent you, locate
   one of their emails, regardless if there is an attachment to that email.
   Once you click an email, Outlook will aggregate all of the sender's
   Outlook items for you using the Outlook People Pane as seen in
   Figure 105.

Wed 7/31/2013 10:58 AM

Bonnie Low-Kramen <bonnielowkramen@gmail.com>

RE: Event page "Tour Schedule"

To ☐ Vickie Sokol Evans

Thanks, Vickie!

Working on it now.

Xo Bon

From: Vickie Sokol Evans [mailto:vevans@redcapeco.com]
Sent: Wednesday, July 31, 2013 10:57 AM
To: Bonnie Low-Kramen

Bonnie Low-Kramen
Instructor Ultimate PA Chicago Feb 2012

ALL	☐ FW: Training Proposal for Amazon	9 hours ago
	↩ RE: Mon July 14	9 hours ago
WHAT'S NEW	🇫 **Bonnie Low-Kramen** 20 min worth the watch. Excellent!	9 hours ago
MAIL	**Full Speech: Jim Carrey's Commencement Address at the 2014 MUM Graduation** www.youtube.com	
ATTACHMENTS	Maharishi University of Management (http://www.mum.edu) granted degrees to 285 students representing 54 countries. Jim Carrey gave the commencement address to Maharishi University of Management's class of	
MEETINGS	2014. The University Board of Trustees also presented Mr. Carrey with the honorary degree of Doctor of Fine Arts Honoris Causa, in recognition...	
	🔲 **Bonnie Low-Kramen** is now connected to **Christine Donohue-Kraynak**	10 hours ago

Figure 105. People Pane - All Tab

2. Click **Attachments** in the People Pane to view all attachments from the sender you have selected.

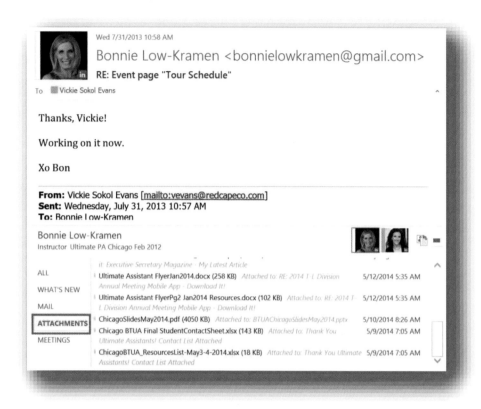

Figure 106. Outlook People Pane - Attachments Tab

3. Click the name of the attachment to launch the email which includes the selected attachment.

In Outlook 2010, click the paperclip icon in the People Pane to view all attachments from the sender you have selected, then double-click the attachment to launch the original email.

The following is a list of additional settings or features of the People Pane. See Figure 107.

1. **Toggle between views** - You can toggle between pictures (of everyone on the email thread) and the People Pane tabs.

2. **Collapse & Expand button** – Rather than go to View tab > People Pane group > People Pane and choose Normal or Minimized, you can use this Collapse & Expand button to Collapse or Display the People Pane.

3. **Social media posts** – If you have the Social Connector enabled, you can view the most recent Facebook and LinkedIn

posts for the email recipient (depending on your connection and on their privacy settings). If your company allows it, to turn this feature on, go to the **View** tab, in the **People Pane** group, click **People Pane**, and then click **Account Settings**. Select the **Connect to a Social Network** to configure your Facebook and LinkedIn connections as seen in Figure 108.

Note: if you don't see the People Pane group on your ribbon or the Account Settings option, your company has most likely disabled this feature.

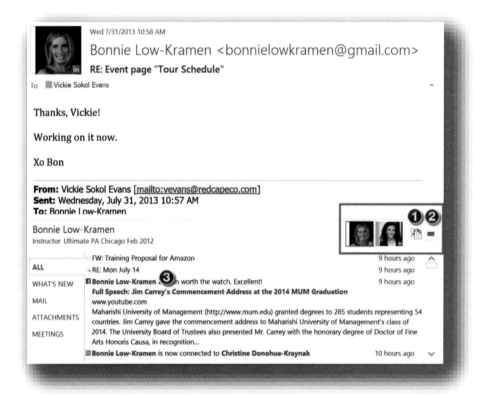

Figure 107. People Pane Settings and Features

Figure 108. Outlook People Pane - Social Connector Settings

Automate your work.

Tip #99 Use Quick Steps to quickly email your project team

Applies to Outlook 2010, Outlook 2013

In Outlook 2010, many new automation features were introduced and are still available to offer one-click access to many common Outlook tasks such as:

- Addressing an email to a team
- Forwarding a message to your manager
- Replying to a message and sending the original to the deleted items
- ...and more!

To use a Quick Step to send a message to a project team

1. In your inbox, on the **Home** tab, in the **Quick Steps** group, click **Team Email**.

2. If you have already configured this button, a new message launches automatically addressed to your team. If not, you will be required to configure the Quick Step the first time you use it as seen in Figure 109.

Figure 109. First Time Setup dialog box for Team Email Quick Step

3. In the **First Time Setup** dialog box, rename the Quick Step, if necessary. For instance, **[Project name] Team Email**.

4. Select your project team members by clicking on the **To...** button, then type each email address in the field. Use the Address book button to look up and confirm names.

Figure 110. Email addresses added to the Team Email First Time Setup dialog box

5. Click **Save**.
6. To use the Quick Step, click on the Quick Step you just created, which will launch a new email message to the team.

 Once your Quick Step is configured, you can modify it by right-clicking the Quick Step and choosing **Edit**.

Tip #100   Resend a message to a different person

Applies to Outlook 2007, Outlook 2010, Outlook 2013

When you want to send the same message to anther recipient you can do that in Outlook using the Resend command, which allows you to address a previously sent email to someone else.

To resend a message to a different person

1. Navigate to your Sent Items folder and double-click the message you want to resend.
2. On the **Message** tab, in the **Move** group, click the **Actions** button, and then select **Resend this Message**.
3. Delete the previous recipient from the message and add the new recipient.

4. Make any necessary changes to the content of the message.
5. When you have completed your changes, click **Send**. Then close the original message.

Notes

Notes